ASTRAL TRAVEL

ASTRAL TRAVEL

Your Guide to the Secrets of Out-of-the-Body Experiences

Gavin and Yvonne Frost

SAMUEL WEISER, INC.

York Beach, Maine

First American edition published in 1986 by
Samuel Weiser, Inc.
Box 612
York Beach, ME 03910

02 01 00 99 98 97 96 95
13 12 11 10 9 8 7

First published in 1982 by
Granada Publishing Ltd., Great Britain

Library of Congress Catalog Card Number: 85-52006

ISBN 0-87728-336-2
MG

Printed in the United States of America

Contents

This book is dedicated to those who have contributed their loving time and effort to this project, and to those who in the future will share their results with the research team. We encourage you to complete the questionnaires in Appendix A at the back of this book and submit your findings to the following address. So as not to destroy this volume, your findings should be submitted on a separate sheet of paper.

If you wish to further your studies in these areas, we invite you to contact:

The School of Wicca
PO Box 1502
New Bern, North Carolina 28560

Introduction

When did you last have that tantalizing experience of having 'been here' before? It happens to everyone. The barely remembered fragment of a 'dream' suddenly takes on form and substance. It is real – but how can such a thing be? This book, in plain simple language, will show you how to remember 'dream' experiences and use them to gain understanding, peace and serenity.

During the past decade more than a thousand people have been involved in the research. From their tens of thousands of reports has come this small volume. The long years of research and cross-correlation of results have culminated in the simple instructions that are contained herein. People from all walks of life, some barely literate, others renowned scholars, have banded together in this selfless effort to push back a final occult frontier of inner space.

Centuries of fear, ignorance and suppression have now given way before the inquiring minds of the dedicated people who make up the research team. In England they still work under the pseudonym of the Canterbury Institute, for even today many of the scholars fear for their reputation and standing in the community if their involvement in occult research were to become known. The only way fear and suppression can be overcome is by the expansion of knowledge: that is why we encourage you to take part in, and report on, your own experiments.

Analysis of team members' reports shows that the Colonel's lady and Rosie O'Grady – in the words of the old song – really are the same under the skin. Not only that, they have the same astral-travel experiences. In every case where researchers' results fell outside the general range of experiences, the deviant results came from people who had extensively studied the subject beforehand and had formed hard and fast preconceived notions of what to expect.

Because the research was done 'cold' by most of the team, a whole range of new phenomena, heretofore unreported, was encountered and cross-correlated between the members of the team. Reading recent texts on the subject of astral travel discloses no mention of these phenomena, though, as you will see in Chapter 9, ancient writings support the existence and the authenticity of these modern findings. Some of the more interesting discoveries are:

HELL DOES NOT EXIST

Despite many attempts by each of the researchers in turn, it was not possible to go to any recognizable area of spiritual torment. Upward and onward, yes; everyone could reach those realms. Downward, back into negativity? No.

ZONAL TIME

In thousands of astral-projection cases it has been found that you cannot project to specific time zones. Instead, you can project only to what might be called 'overlap points' between our present reality and future and past realities.

DISTORTION OF REALITY WITH TIME

Your great-grandfather's mezzotint picture is fading away. In the same manner, when you travel into previous time zones your perception of the scene fades in the mists of the past. Conversely, as you move forward into the future the scene's constituents intensify. Sounds and colours grow more harsh and more bright until eventually they become so strident as to be painful.

REALITY CONTROL

Your ability to affect events varies with the time zone you are in. When you astral project into 'now', you will find that you may be able to turn the page of a book, but you cannot lift the book. You have no power to affect history, but much power to affect events in the future.

SIDE/HEAVEN

Canterbury Institute researchers call the other side of the invisible barrier simply 'Side'. The ancient Irish called it 'Sidhe'. In some ways Side is comparable to heaven; however, most clergy, not having visited it, are unable to convey its actuality to you. After reading this book, you will be able to visit the realm for yourself; for it is a real place that you can explore with equanimity and confidence.

These are but a few of the concepts never before made public. When you begin to apply them in your life, they will enlarge your understanding of the marvellous cosmos in which we all exist.

'Thank You – Now I Know'

The files at Canterbury Institute and at the School of Wicca contain thousands of letters from researchers who felt the impulse to write and thank the team for the unexpected yet very real benefits that the participants gained, in both their mundane and spiritual lives. Typical of these letters is a note received from Irma Bach in Frankfurt, West Germany:

I have never before experienced such serenity and tranquillity. Being an elderly woman (83 my last birthday), I was very worried about what was awaiting me when I died. Now I know. I have no more fear. In fact I am quite looking forward to my transition into the realms of light. I no longer cling to my great-grandchildren, for I know that I will be able to see them forever. I pray every day that your great work will be able to proceed.

Would that all could be so sure of their future. If they were, the world would be better for it.

CHAPTER 1
Enjoy This New Occult Frontier

'In the agonizing moment that seemed to last for ever, that moment before the train hit me, I finally realized this was a serious experiment. Question upon question raced through my astral consciousness. Were Gavin and Yvonne really reliable? Did the Canterbury Institute and the Church and School of Wicca know what they were doing? Was the train going to kill me? Or would I come off unscathed, as they had promised? Was I crazy to place my trust in people I had never met, and in some rather glib statements in some lectures I had received through the mail?

'A few moments later I knew that everything was all right. Yes, the train hit me and my astral body went on a curving upward course through the engine, the tender, and the first freight car. The impact was slight. Just as had been promised, I was light as a feather. Now I was floating above the train with confused memories of moving mechanical parts, gauges, a tank of diesel fuel, interspersed with lots of free space. This experience gave me the confidence to go further into the realms of astral travel, and now I believe I have explored all except the outermost realms of time and the uppermost spiritual domains.

'I cannot thank you, the people at the Canterbury Institute, or the other workers enough for having added these new dimensions to my life. I am a Christian still firmly committed to my faith. Many things I have seen and done have led me to a new understanding of the meaning of the Bible and of Jesus. I can never express my gratitude for all you have done for me; and I wish you well. May the bonds between all religions grow in love.'

The foregoing is an extract from a letter written by a paraplegic veteran. Once he was on the verge of suicide because he was, he thought, condemned for the rest of his natural life to sit in a wheelchair and be tended by others. Astral travel added a new dimension to his life, a dimension where he spends as much time as he can while his body remains in its wheelchair. In addition to the extensive experimental work this man has done for us, many times he has added comments such as, 'If only people knew the truth! If only people would experiment as I have done! Not only would they lose their fear of the astral realms, but they would also have a far more serene life and lose their fear of death and dying.'

You can follow our friend into the astral realms. At the time of writing, even more subjects are conducting experiments for us and in that way are contributing to this work. We believe the instructions we give here are the most comprehensive, the easiest to understand and follow, that have ever been offered to the public. They are not the results of one or two people's by-chance astral trips; they are the result of a large body of trained subjects working with conscious intent for a common end. The participants come from all walks of life, and from all nations of the free world. You can astral travel too. You can do it without fear, for no one in all the thousands of letters and reports that we have on file has ever reported any difficulty.

This book is intended as a practical guide, a book you can use to follow others on to the astral. We recommend that you first read it through to get the general gist and meaning. Then, and most importantly, you should read it a second time and try out the instructions contained in each chapter before proceeding to the next.

Re-evaluating Ancient Knowledge

The Pyramids and the Sphinx of ancient Egypt bear witness to the greatness of the civilization that existed in those far-off days. In Egypt was found the Rhind Papyrus; on that papyrus are inscribed from ancient days all the degrees of latitude from the Equator to the North Pole. With today's modern satellite equipment we find that the Egyptians' knowledge of the planet far surpassed anything they could have been expected to know from the apparent state of their science.

The ancient Mayans produced a calendar more accurate than the one we use today. The Mayans were able to chart the progress of the planets to an accuracy of better than one day in six thousand years. Only since the invention of the atomic crystal clock have modern scientists been able to improve very slightly on the accuracy of the Mayan calendar.

Other cultures in South America also had astounding knowledge and skills. The monumental structures and city buildings made from cut stone by the Incas on the tops of mountains are a well-known enigma that remains to be explained. Modern construction equipment would have difficulty in duplicating the work of the Incas. When viewing those mountain sites, modern contractors shake their heads in wonder and amazement; and despite a millionaire's offer of funding, no contractor has yet been found who would attempt to duplicate the work.

To the north, the Incas' Aztec brothers were pyramid builders. The base measurements of the Pyramid of the Sun near Mexico City are identical to the base measurements of the Great Pyramid of Gizeh in Egypt.

In England ancient peoples built great stone or 'megalithic' monuments to a very exact measure which astro-archaeologists call the 'megalithic yard'. That measure is based on the foot, which is not, as many suppose, derived from the anatomy of some long-dead king but is, instead, an astronomically perfect measure.[1]

There are many other common beliefs shared by peoples who were separated from one another by thousands of miles. Various theorists have propounded different hypotheses for the very sophisticated scientific knowledge displayed by ancient peoples. In recent years the ancient-astronaut theory has received a lot of attention. In our opinion, there may indeed have been ancient astronauts; however, astral travel seems to us to be a far easier way for knowledge to have been transmitted from one ancient civilization to another.

It is our premise that this knowledge came from astral guidance and that the peoples involved knew the realms where they could contact higher beings and get information from them. In support of this theory, ancient Egyptian writings clearly show that they had knowledge of astral travel and that in healing they regularly separated the patient's consciousness from his mundane body so the patient would feel no pain while healing was being accomplished. Thus astral projection seems to have been an ancient universal experience important enough to be recorded in early writings.

During the Middle Ages men began to scoff at astral experiences; such experiences were not sanctioned by state-controlled religions. At about the same time, eastern meditation was changed. No longer was the meditator allowed to float free (astral project); instead he was ordered to concentrate on a single mantra. Later in 'scientific' western countries astral experiences were laughed at and then ruthlessly suppressed by the newly educated 'rational' middle class. Because of world-wide suppression of those experiences, the source of infinite knowledge available to the Ancients was

---

[1] It is based on the length of a degree of latitude at Winchester, the old British capital near Stonehenge. One degree of latitude divided by the length of the year in days times 1,000 gives the foot to four places of decimals.

lost to us. Only in the last decade or so, with the new legitimacy of astral travel and its scientific testing by such people as Dr Charles Tart of the University of California at Davis, has it become acceptable.

With the aid of this book, you too can tap into the knowledge that enriched the life of the Ancients: astral knowledge which can be of vital importance in your growth today. Do not try to evaluate astral travel with cold logic, for if you do you will miss the whole point. The astral reality is not necessarily a logical place in terms of the physical world. We urge you to try the experiments we suggest. Experience controlled astral travel for yourself. Expand your awareness. Then judge the results for yourself.

The Light-Hearted Side of Astral Travel

Astral projection, or more simply, letting your spirit travel without your body, is one of the most useful and entertaining skills you can ever learn. You can watch others in their daily lives facing and overcoming problems; you can learn what other people honestly think of you; you can find out what really happened in history – and what is to happen in the future.

In their private lives people do the most amazing and amusing things. The serious, staid pillar of the community is often one of the most relaxed people you could ever wish to meet when he is in his own home. People have to relax sometimes, and it seems that those who are the most uptight, the most self-conscious on the outside, are the most amusing when off guard. You can see life as it actually is. You can have great fun taking the starch out of your local vicar, perhaps by commenting in an offhand way on his most private and amusing habits. That bank manager who's giving you a hard time over your loan will be infinitely more relaxed with you if you can talk to him about his favourite hobby.

You will not only know what his hobby is, but will also know exactly how he feels about it.

You Have Already Astral Travelled!

You may doubt this startling claim, but you can prove it for yourself tonight. Demand an answer from your mind to a question whose answer you cannot possibly know. The question can be as simple as, 'What type of house does X live in?' having picked the X at random from the telephone directory. Write down the first thing you feel about X's house when you wake. Now phone X. On your first attempt you may find that X is unco-operative; but if you present it as a wager, most people will go along with the gag.

The *déjà vu* (having been here before) experience is another common way you can prove to yourself that you have genuinely had astral-travel experiences. In most *déjà vu* cases, you get 'the feeling' just before you enter a room or go round a corner. Write down what you think you are going to see, or tell someone about it. Then walk round the corner. Now you can prove that you actually have been there before. Since in many cases it was totally impossible for you to have been there in the body, you have proved once again that astral travel is real.

You have already spontaneously astral travelled during sleep. Now, through following step by step the instructions in these pages, your trips can be directed instead of random, useful instead of pointless. The purpose of this book is to show you how to control and use those previously unplanned trips.

Two Life-and-Death Cases

In the files we have many documented cases of people who effortlessly learned to astral travel. Some of these people became students because of the vivid but unexplainable things that happened to them − unexplainable, that is, in terms of their orthodox religious background. Here are two cases in which astral projection meant the difference between life and death.

Case 1 − Harry J.

Harry J. is a Missouri farmer. On his land there are many limestone cave formations. One day his twelve-year-old son persuaded Harry to take him into one of the caves. Neither Harry nor Bucky knew very much about speleology, the science of cave exploration; they just grabbed a couple of torches and a rope, and went off down into the caves. They got lost. They had no compass, and pretty soon the batteries in their torches began to fail. Wisely, they sat down to await rescue. Meanwhile on the surface a heavy storm broke out, and in the cave where they sat the water quickly began to rise. In this situation Bucky panicked. He began to run away from the water. Harry grabbed at him but slipped and hit his head on a rock. He found himself free of his body. As he recounts it, the cave that had been pitch-dark was now eerily illuminated. In his new state he 'knew' the way out and he drifted out through the entrance of the cave. A few moments later he regained consciousness back in his body. Now, even in the dark and in the rushing waters, he was able to guide Bucky through the maze of caves safely back to the entrance.

Case 2 − Helga N.

Helga N. lives in a flat in Munich. A thalidomide baby, she does not have the use of her legs. Perhaps as a kind of compensation Helga has the ability to spontaneously astral travel.

Normally her mother and father would be in the flat; but Helga convinced them she would be all right with her friend

Kaethe while the parents went skiing in the Bavarian Alps. She knew they would benefit by a brief time away from the responsibilities that stemmed from her handicap.

Helga and Kaethe were having a pleasant weekend when Kaethe's mother called to say that her father had had a stroke. Could Kaethe come home, she urged, because the doctors did not expect him to last the night. Kaethe and Helga talked things over; Helga assured Kaethe she would be quite all right, provided only that Kaethe help her into bed. Kaethe did this and rushed off to her father's bedside.

During the night fire broke out in a flat adjacent to Helga's. Thick choking smoke soon woke Helga. She coughed and cried out, but no one came, for the block of flats was built in solid German fashion and sounds were not easily transmitted through the walls. Realizing her fate lay in her own hands, Helga astral projected herself and searched for someone who could be made aware of her plight. First she went to Kaethe, but Kaethe was so wrapped up in the crisis at her home that Helga could not get her attention. Helga tried other people she knew, but everywhere she turned they seemed to be busy. Finally she had an inspiration. She rushed back to Kaethe's house and contacted Kaethe's father as he lay there. With almost his last breathe he told Kaethe of Helga's danger and urged her to rescue her helpless friend. Helga watched as Kaethe got her coat and took the *Strassenbahn* (streetcar) to the block of flats, where she saved Helga's earth-plane life.

How This Book Can Guide You to a Better Life

Do these examples seem far-fetched? They are not. Our files contain hundreds of similar examples of people from all walks of life who have gained by learning to astral project.

Whether you know it or not, you yourself lead a double life. The life you live in the world where you earn your living is matched with a similar life you live on the other side of the invisible barrier that divides the astral world from the earth plane. Many people claim they do not live in that mysterious other half of life, and they sincerely believe they do not. By getting them to try the techniques spelled out in these pages, we showed them that they do actually live in both worlds. Your life in the plane of existence where you are reading this information today may be chaotic or painful for you, but what is your life like in the astral? Upon examination you may find that your astral life is near perfect. All you need to do is match your astral to your earth-plane life to bring the perfection of your astral to the earth plane and

OVERCOME MANY OF THE EVERYDAY PROBLEMS YOU MAY HAVE.

It works the other way too. If your mundane life is unsatisfactory, but you can't work out why, you may find that you have some problems in the astral realms. Checking on the astral for problems is an essential part of any attempt to make your life serene and happy.

Astral Projection Will Work for You

Do you dream?

OF COURSE YOU DO!

Do you daydream?

OF COURSE YOU DO!

Can you imagine yourself in a different place doing something different?

OF COURSE YOU CAN!

When you do these things, you are ALREADY doing all

that will be required of you in this book. By simply extending your dream sequences and programming them, you will be able to astral project. Many people do not realize how often 'dreams' are actually astral projections. For that reason and because the dream state is the easiest from which to astral project, we are going to digress for a few pages to discuss dreams.

Everyone Dreams

You dreamed last night. You may not have any memory of the dreams you had, but modern research clearly shows that everyone dreams. Whether you remember it or not, you dreamed. There are two basic reasons that may be preventing you from remembering your dreams:

1. Too tired to remember – When you go to bed exhausted, you go into a deep sleep state. In this state you dream, but the veil between the conscious and the unconscious minds is tightly drawn. The conscious mind is busy helping the body recover from its exhaustion and repairing tissues. Signals from the lower levels of the mind cannot be comprehended while the upper portions of the mind are preoccupied.

2. Unexpected impressions – Many people expect only to see pictures when they dream, but people don't dream in pictures. Instead the impressions they get come as:
   a. sounds – This mode of dreaming is called 'auditory'. Psychics refer to people who are open to sound messages as 'clairaudients'.
   b. smells – Unusual as this may seem, it is a recognized mode of receiving dream impressions called nowadays 'olfactory'.
   c. taste – Have you ever woken up with a bad taste in your mouth that is not related to overindulgence at

supper-time the night before? The phrase 'left a bad taste in my mouth' is the unwitting acknowledgment that people do in fact receive inputs through their sense of taste or 'tastition'.

d. emotion – When you first meet a person, even before so much as a handshake or a word has been exchanged, you have feelings about him. When you enter a house it can feel friendly or cold, or may give you some other impression. Occasionally you may awake with strong emotional feelings that something (either good or bad) is about to happen. This 'sentition' is a recognized and highly valuable method of dreaming.

The notable missing sense in the list above is your sense of touch, or 'tactition'. While you are sleeping many outside environmental influences affect such things as the temperature of the room and the feel of the sheets against your body, and Canterbury Institute research has shown that for this reason tactition is not a reliable conveyor of dream information.

Even though you may not see pictures, i.e. are not 'voyant', you still dream. Whenever you awake with something on the surface of one of your senses that was not there when you went to sleep, it is most likely that this sensation is the result of your subconscious communicating to your consciousness in the sleep state.

There Is No Such Thing as a 'Bad' Dream

Remember the time you woke up sweating and afraid, absolutely sure that 'it' was going to get you? Did you hate the feeling? Can you now understand that the nightmare was a very serious attempt by your subconscious to communicate important guidance to you? Most people assume that unpleasant dreams are 'bad' and pleasant dreams are 'good'.

This arbitrary categorization of dreams becomes meaningless when you realize that almost all dreams are directed by your own mind.

Once you have overcome the emotion that the dream engendered in you, you need to look for the dream's real message. What did the 'it' that was after you really symbolize? Was it a friend concealing hatred and planning to do the dirty on you? Was it the bank manager who will be after you if you don't straighten out your financial problems? Was it your room-mate whose actions threaten your sexuality or serenity? The nightmare was trying to tell you something, and you need to decide what that something is. Conversely, you may have a lovely lighthearted dream about running through a field of fragrant flowers. Suddenly you have to leave this pleasant place. There is no real pressure in the dream, but there is a sense of loss. You may not awake with any heavy emotional feeling; you may forget the dream rather quickly. Yet this dream may have just as serious a message to communicate as the nightmare had.

The important thing to remember is that no dream is random or meaningless. In your search for serenity and a smooth path through life, every dream deserves equal consideration.

Dream Guidance

The guidance you receive from dreams is not limited to problem-solving in your personal life. It can be used to solve any sort of problem – personal, mundane or spiritual – that you are wrestling with. Successful executives always 'sleep on' major decisions. Many famous inventors have used dreams to perfect their discoveries. Dream guidance is one way by which many unknown and relatively poorly-educated people have become millionaires through unusual but important inventions. Countless scientists give credit for some of their most spectacular discoveries to their dream messages. It is well known that Thomas Edison slept in a chair in his lab so that he could immediately try out any ideas he got from his dreams. The discoverer of the benzene ring, Professor Kugel, got the idea through a dream. Without his discovery, organic chemistry would not exist. These cases are by no means isolated. The sewing machine, the DNA molecule and the bicycle are all documented cases of dream discoveries. In many cases this knowledge embodied ideas that were new to the inventor and to the world. Where did this knowledge come from?

It is the firm belief of both the writers and the researchers at the Canterbury Institute that the knowledge came from the astral realms. Work at the Institute has shown that once you have your mundane life ordered and serene, you can begin using your sleep time to answer any question that you may have, no matter to what it applies.

Guidance from Within

Neurosurgeons have long known that in daily living you use only a small percentage of your mind's capacity. Your mind is a miraculous problem-solver, one whose capabilities are only just being comprehended. It is far better at solving your problems than is a giant computer or an outside counsellor. You have within you what is sometimes called your own 'Indwelling Sage'. That Sage is your brain. It has more information stored in its memory banks than you can possibly realize. You have heard, no doubt, of how hypnosis can unlock the memories that are deep within the mind. Similarly, during sleep you can get in touch with all those levels of memory where everything you have ever seen or learned is stored.

The material that you have stored in your mind does not necessarily correlate with the way you received your educa-

tion. Every day as you walk around, your senses pick up
information. Often this information is absorbed at a sub-
liminal (below conscious awareness) level. Even though you
may have done badly at school and never passed a single
exam in your life, within your brain all the scholastic
knowledge you were ever exposed to is still stored.

When you start asking your mind to answer specific questions during sleep, you are harnessing the power of your total
consciousness. You take charge of what you are going to
dream about. You request information and help, and your
mind gives you the answer or shows you how to obtain the
information you have requested. Because you have placed it
in the upper levels of your consciousness, the one thing your
mind cannot do is ignore your request. Until the request is
fulfilled, your subconscious cannot communicate any other
information to you.

Guidance from Without

When your mind does not have the answer that you need, it
will direct your consciousness to a place where such an
answer can be obtained. There is a whole realm of knowledge
and wisdom that you are able to tap. Sometimes that realm is
called the 'universal unconscious'. Scientifically orientated
people tend to call it the 'great computer in the sky'. Children
refer to it as a 'fairy godmother'. Knowledge of the realm's
existence is universal, though mostly unmentioned. You can
get answers to questions from this realm through your
directed consciousness and in this way answer questions
whose solutions you could have had no possible way of
knowing. Such problem-solving clearly shows that you can
communicate with sources of information which are beyond
those within your own mind.

When you urgently need an answer to a question, part of
you – the part we call the spirit – detaches itself from your

body and travels independently to find the answers you need. Such independent travel and the finding of answers to problems or questions that you had no knowledge of is simple, straightforward astral projection. Many cases of it have been well documented by impartial observers. In the eighteenth century, Dr Swedenborg in Göteborg, Sweden, reported the minute-by-minute progress of a disastrous fire in Stockholm, 300 miles away. As a result of this experience, Swedenborg taught others how to astral project and in fact formed a new world-wide church, all of whose ministers have astral-projection ability.

In the USA, as recently as April 1980, there was a documented film report on NBC television of a girl who accurately described the interior of a house in California, even though she had never visited the state or met the people who lived in the house. Moreover, this twelve-year-old girl was blind. As in Helga's case, astral travel is a compensation for her disability.

Extending Your Life with Astral Travel

In today's world, when you sleep you are assumed to be 'wasting' your time. After all, it looks as if you are lying there accomplishing nothing. Yet without sleep you would become irritable, then ill and, finally, you might even die. So you must have sleep. Now, though, you can USE that sleep time, extending your life from this plane of existence into a totally new – better – reality, a place where you can be active while you sleep and can have more fun than you do here. Say that you are confined to a wheelchair or that you have to stay in bed for some reason. There is nothing to stop you from going into a reality that is just as valid as this one and exploring the realm on the other side of the invisible barrier. As you proceed into that other reality, you will find that it is populated with people just as this plane is. Some of the people are beautiful and friendly, and some are ugly and unpleasant. In the astral reality, however, it is easier to avoid the negative beings than it is in the earth plane; for they make themselves known very clearly by their muddy-coloured auras.

You can have a whole life on the other side. The first time you make love in the astral, you will be amazed at how satisfying and completing that melding experience is. Afterwards you may be haunted by the lack of completion you feel in making love on this plane.

You will learn to make earth-plane time meaningless and enter other realities that exist at higher levels of development than the one to which you normally go. You can range over cosmic distances in the blink of an eye.

You can do it now! Sit now and think yourself on to the moon. Feel the cold; see the loneliness; look at the jagged craters; listen to the silence. Your mind travels faster than any future starship ever will. Indeed the range of your astral self is limited only by what you will it to do. Your astral-travelling self can go anywhere and can do anything. Before you go to bed tonight, decide where you would like to go in your very first planned trip. Write down the place. In most cases you will visit it while you 'sleep'.

Visit the Past, Present and Future

Astral travel extends the scope of your life. Even today, when you are free of your body in dreams you can have experiences that in other circumstances would be considered beyond credibility. You can be a king in his palace or a sheikh in a harem. You can make love to the most beautiful women in the world; or as the queen of all you survey, you can be courted by the most romantic and attractive man it is possible to imagine. Whether you are rich or poor you can travel in time to see the past and the future. You can go at no cost to any place in the cosmos. We will also teach you to travel into other realms – realms and realities beyond the known cosmos, realms impossible to reach without this training. You can bring back knowledge about the future and about other ways that will be of inestimable benefit to you in your present life.

With the aid of the astral Little People (for little people really do exist) you will become able to find that proverbial pot of gold at the end of the rainbow. Age, upbringing, education – all totally irrelevant. Although we have found that it is slightly more difficult for a white Christian to accomplish all that others can, this difficulty is so easily overcome by the Institute's techniques as to be almost non-existent. If you devote a few of those Sundays you would normally spend in church to the practice of these techniques, you will find that you can accomplish just as much as any other citizen of the world.

Calm Your Fears with Astral Travel

Many people are afraid they will meet harmful bogeymen or strange monsters on the other side of the barrier. Those fears are totally groundless. Yes, you will meet some odd-looking characters from time to time; but they cannot harm you. Come: Have you ever considered whether a ghost or spirit can be harmed? *It just isn't possible!* No more can you be harmed when you are travelling the astral realms. Once you know what the other side of the barrier is really like, you will no longer fear such things as death or spirits. Then you will gain tremendous serenity and calm.

Summary

Exploring astral realms is not only safe; it is also most rewarding. From the safety of your own home you can visit any location you wish. The places you visit are limited only by your own desires. The knowledge you gain from your travels will not only aid you in your immediate, present life, but will also give you greater understanding of the underlying reasons why things happen as they do.

You may often have asked yourself: 'Why am I alive?' or 'What am I doing here?' Soon, as you complete the astral-travel exercises in this book, you will have your own answers to these ageless questions, questions that the wisest philosophers have sought to answer for centuries.

When you astral travel, you will infinitely expand your knowledge of the cosmic realities in which all exists.

CHAPTER 2
Astral Dreaming

Is the other half of life passing you by? Are you missing out on the opportunity to explore, from the safety of your own home, the world of the astral? This chapter will show you how to start immediately exploring other planes of existence and other realities.

In your everyday speech you yourself acknowledge that you are part of a 'twin'. You say, 'I love', 'I feel', 'I need' – then, perhaps in the next breath, you speak of 'My arm', 'My body'. The 'I' is the real you, the astral consciousness that lives for ever. 'Me' is only the shell you are temporarily inhabiting.

Throughout recorded history, the fact has been known that all living beings are composed of an astral and a mundane part. The Rig Veda, the ancient holy book of the Hindus said to date from 2000 BCE[1], states that a human being is like a driver in a chariot: the chariot is your body, the 'Me', and the driver is your astral consciousness, the 'I'. The driver can leave the chariot for as long as he or she wishes. If the chariot gets wrecked, the 'I'-driver can leave permanently, either to dwell in the astral realms or to return and get a new chariot for itself. In western civilizations this changing of one chariot for another is called 'death'.

With their concepts of Ka (the astral double) and Ba (the spirit) the Egyptians showed a very advanced knowledge of the parts of a being some 6,000 years ago. Their literature acknowledges the fact that the Ka and the Ba can leave the earth-plane shell 'Me' at will. The occult underground in the western world has freely acknowledged the fact of this duality

[1] 'Before Common Era'.

and has retained knowledge of how to separate the two halves of any living being.

You Astral Project Every Night

When you start recording your dreams, you will notice that they fall into definite categories.

Category 1 – Observer Dreams. You are outside and apart from the dream. You are sitting in a cinema viewing the action as it passes before you. You should pay close attention, for the scene may contain an omen or a portent that will help you in your life.[2]

Category 2 – Participant Dreams. In these you are actively present; usually, though, you are being tormented in some way. The torment may range from something very mild to an all-out crisis or pursuit by some unknown terror. Such dreams tend to become nightmarish. They are signs that something is definitely amiss in your life and needs correcting. When you have one of these dreams, if you can, remember that it is *your* dream and you can change it in any way you wish. If it becomes too nightmarish, stop. Say to yourself, 'This is ridiculous. I'm doing it to myself.' Or, 'I've got the message and I'll fix my life tomorrow.' When you think in this way and the dream scene obeys your command, it is a true dream.

Category 3 – These are participant dreams, but you are not in control.

THESE ARE NOT DREAMS – THEY ARE ASTRAL TRIPS

This type of dream occurs every night. Our researchers call them 'A-state dreams'. In them you are actually astral travell-

[2]For further discussions of this subject, see Gavin and Yvonne Frost, *A Witch's Grimoire of Ancient Omens, Portents, Talismans, Amulets, and Charms*, published by Parker Publishing Company.

ing. One of the ways in which you can tell the difference between a Category 2 and a Category 3 dream is that in the Category 2 you have full control over events around you. You can stop the oncoming car. You can turn the tap on and off. In Category 3 astral travel, you have little or no control over events around you. If you stand in the path of an oncoming car, it will pass right through you. The car is a real vehicle going somewhere and, unlike the situation in a Category 2 dream, you cannot stop it.

You will not be harmed in any way by the experience because your astral is not a thing of flesh and blood. The car exists in a different plane of reality than your astral self.

When you astral travel into the present real world, the here-now, you can make your presence felt in very minor ways. Experiments have shown that the astral body actually weighs something in the order of 56 grams (2 oz). If you can imagine things that would be affected by something that weighs so little, these are the things you can make happen. In other words, you can turn the pages of a book but you cannot lift the book. When we discuss other places that you will go in astral travel, we will tell you what you can and cannot expect to be able to make happen in them. In each of the realms we will show you how to visit, there are general cosmic rules which you cannot flout.

In the here-now realm you will find you can pass through physically existing objects such as your bedroom wall and things like cars can pass through you. The here-now world is populated with real people going about their mundane business – and these too will pass right through you.

It is also populated with other astral beings. These beings appear solid to your astral body because you and they are on the same plane of existence. When your astral self tries to pass through another astral being, in contrast to 'real' or mundane people, you feel the impact as you bump into them.

Relationships can be formed on the astral. If anything, these are even more fulfilling than those in the everyday world. This is particularly true in cases of sexual relationships, which are totally guilt-free, fulfilling and exquisite.

Understanding Astral Projection

It used to be said that witches flew on broomsticks to meet their fellows. Modern research has shown that in a sense this is true. They did 'fly' with the aid of a broomstick – which was apparently coated with a hallucinogenic 'flying ointment' that allowed the witch readily to dissociate the two halves of her being. Many people in the drug subculture have learned to use the term 'trip out', for they too can separate their astral consciousness from their mundane body through the use of certain substances.

Before the end of this book you should be able to separate the two halves of your being at will without the use of drugs. This is not to say that in the early days you will be able to do it every time you try. Gradually, as you do it more and more often, just like practice in any endeavour, your success rate will improve. Remember, you are already separating your two halves at least once every night.

Your total problem in astral projection, therefore, is that you retain no memory of tripping out. The forgetting of astral travel is often coupled with a lack of dream memory. Scientists have conclusively demonstrated that everyone dreams during at least three periods every night. If you think you do not dream, it is because you do not remember them, not because you don't have the experience.

Exactly the same thing is true of astral projection. Our experiments show that most people astral travel at least once every night, though only a very small percentage of these people remember where they went or what they did.

The first skill you need to learn, then, is to remember your dreams; it is a learned skill, easy to acquire, a skill that anyone can master.

Remembering Your Dreams and Astral Trips

If you habitually burn the candle at both ends and go to bed exhausted, you will sleep so heavily that you will remember neither dreams nor astral trips. If you habitually go to bed tense and frustrated, bound up with personal conflicts, the only dreams you will have are those dealing with the problems. So the first two rules in remembering dreams are:

1. Get plenty of sleep: for good dreams, at least ten hours a night.
2. Don't go to bed with a lot of personal problems on your mind, or even right after watching a film or television programme that involves violence and gore.

This is a classic chicken-and-egg situation: astral travel can help you in your life – but your life must be ordered enough so you can learn to astral travel before such travel can help! Sometimes indeed we have found people who cannot remember their first astral trip until this pattern is broken. If you have trouble with these directions, we recommend that you take a week's holiday at the seaside or in the country. There you will find that recollection becomes easier.

About the Interpretation of Dreams

Most people dream and travel in pictures, as if they were in an ongoing film. We find that these people do not fully remember sounds, smells, tastes or emotional states from their sleeping time.

Similarly those people who are orientated to a sense other than sight have poor ability to remember visions. The remem-

brance of other sensory inputs varies greatly from subject to
subject. Many remember such emotions as terror from a
nightmare, but have no recollection of emotions like love.
Eventually you can train yourself to remember all your
sensory inputs.

Imagine you are at a football match. A player has just
scored a goal. Everyone leaps to his feet and cheers. When
you think of this scene, do you see it? Hear it? Smell the
people? Feel those near to you pushing against you? Or feel
the emotion generated in the stand? Whichever way you
respond will be the way that you should emphasize first in
developing your dream recall, for it is the primary way in
which your mind thinks. With an effort of will you can
visualize, hear and feel the emotion of the football match.
Work at it longer and you can smell, taste and feel the
physical pressure of other people. In just the same way after
you have learned to retain your primary form of astral
sensory input, so you can then develop your capabilities and
recall secondary inputs. Among the various types of primary
sensory awareness, the percentage breakdown is:

90% see pictures	Clairvoyance
6% feel things and wake up 'in a mood'	Clairsentience
1% taste things and awaken with a good or a bad flavour	Clairgustation
1% smell things; the bad-smell phenomenon	Clairolfaction
2% hear things; 'somebody told me'	Clairaudience

Your Internal Symbology

Your dreams are your own personal creations. The symbols
you see in them are created by your own mind; they are
unique to your individual background and experience. It is

true than many common symbols are universally recognized. In dreams the symbols are uniquely personal and cannot readily be interpreted by a third party unless that third party is able to explore with the dreamer the meaning of the symbols the dreamer saw. An example: to many people who live away from the seaside, a dream of seagulls would be taken as a positive thing rather than the very negative imagery it gives to people like us, who live with the messes gulls create. This is why we cannot 'read' dreams by mail for people who write to us. There must be that essential personal interchange so that the meaning *in your reality* of the symbology you saw can be made clear.

Not only that, but on an almost minute-to-minute basis, your own symbology changes. You are in the street, where you see an accident involving a blue car. In your own mind, subtle changes have now been made in your feelings about the colour blue. From a quiet, cool colour of peace, it has abruptly become a reminder of death and destruction.

Often we are asked to interpret dreams and scenes which people have viewed while astral travelling. The big difference between dreams and astral travel is this: in astral travel the scenes you observe are real. They have actually happened, will happen, or are occurring in other planes of existence; therefore they need no interpretation.

The External Reality

When you astral travel, you are voyaging to real places. In your first astral trips these will most likely be in your own neighbourhood in the present time-frame. There are differences between the astral present and the physical present, but those differences do not involve symbology. You are seeing[3] what is literally there.

[3]Throughout the rest of this book, we shall use 'seeing'; as a generic term to include seeing, feeling, hearing, smelling, etc.; that is, for all the means of receiving impressions.

No Need to Be Afraid

We often receive letters at the School from people who are afraid of learning to remember their dreams, afraid of astral travelling, afraid of separating their 'I' from their 'Me'. They explain fearfully that they talked to their minister about it and he forbade them to proceed. Yet the Bible speaks clearly on the subject. The separation of the spirit from the body is clearly defined in Genesis; and in II Corinthians 12, Paul speaks even more clearly of astral projection: 'I know a Christian man who fourteen years ago ... was caught up as far as the third heaven and ... into Paradise and heard words so secret that human lips may not repeat them.'

The existence and practice of astral travel is proved beyond the shadow of a doubt, not only by the hundreds of documented cases and by the thousands of letters we receive each year, but also by our own experiences and those of the research team.

'No, You're Not Dead'

An incident from the life of one of our researchers demonstrates how beneficial knowledge of the astral plane can be:

'When I was about six years old I attended kindergarten school at a big old house in Walsall. One day when I was returning from the rest room I slipped and fell down the long flight of stairs that connected the classroom to the upper storeys of the house. I remember sitting on the top step and watching my body being taken away by an ambulance attendant. I was totally terrified. I had no idea what was happening to me. I knew little or nothing about death, and in fact I knew I wasn't dead because I was sitting on the top step! How could I possibly be dead? Yet those people down there at the bottom of the stairs were taking *my* body away! I was very angry with them for doing it; but since the headmistress was there, I could do nothing. For even speaking to the headmistress in those days was an act far beyond my stature. After a little while of sitting there, an elderly man came and sat by my side. He was dressed in a painter's overall. He said his name was Al. He didn't actually speak to me, yet somehow he did. I told Al how annoyed I was that those people had stolen my body. Al assured me that I would get it back. He seemed very sad and I asked him why he was so sure I would get my body back. I will always remember his answer: "Because you're not dead yet. I am dead. I just fell off my ladder across the street." The next thing I remember was waking up in my body. I assume now that I was scared of Al, for he must have been a 'ghost', and ghosts in those days were scary things. In fact later investigation showed that Al fell from the ladder at almost the same moment that I fell down the stairs and in fact all I had really done was knock myself out for a few moments. I really had no one to tell my experience to, and with time it faded.

'It seems as though in my youth I was always prone to accidents of this sort. On another occasion I was sledging on a wooded slope when one of the sledge runners came off. Now out of control, the sledge smashed into a tree, the same tree which my mundane body hit with its head. On this occasion "I" landed in the snow on the other side of the tree. Again, my body was briefly unconscious, and I was separated from it. This time I was less scared, but still had no idea of how to get back into my body. After a momentary blank I found myself sitting up in my body with a terrible pain in my head and blood running down my face.

'Again on another occasion I was carrying a roll of wire netting down a ladder from a farm loft, and overbalanced backwards. This time "I" stayed on the ladder and watched the body – my body – hit the ground, breaking its arm in its fall. I instantly felt its pain in my astral arm.'

Canterbury Institute research shows that when the astral consciousness knows the body is going to hit something, it hangs back, letting the body go on, even presumably to accident site. In thousands of cases in occult literature you will astral consciousness is fooled so that when the body is abruptly stopped, the astral consciousness continues on its old path and ends up free of the body on the other side of the accident site. In thousands of cases in occult literature you find many data on these types of astral separation.

Piercing the Astral Veil

Very few people are fortunate – or unfortunate – enough to be involved in minor accidents of the type that the researcher remembers so well. We suspect that in days gone by, when more people lived in rural areas and did more actual physical work, accidents of these kinds occurred more often and people were more aware of their astral body than they are today, when the environments of many people are nearly free of hazards. Because he pierced the Veil, our researcher became aware at a very young age that separation of the astral consciousness from the mundane body was possible and not to be feared.

That same veil prevents you remembering your dreams. Only when you take special measures can you remember all your dreams and avail yourself of the knowledge they contain. If the veil is not deliberately removed, it conceals from you knowledge you could use to good advantage. When the veil is torn aside, as it is in thousands of cases, you begin to see that life holds more than those things the mundane body, 'Me', experiences.

You have probably had the experience of waking up after a particularly vivid dream in something of an emotional state, whether fear, desire or anger. Even the following morning you can clearly remember waking up – but have absolutely no recall of *why*. If questioned, you are quite unable to describe the dream that interrupted your sleep. The Veil has closed. If you take a moment when you wake up to write down three or four significant factors from the dream, on the following morning you will find you can retell the dream in full detail. You have succeeded in lifting the Veil at least a little.

To Sleep, to Dream, to Astral Travel

In 1953 a new breakthrough in dream research occurred: the correlation of rapid eye movement (REM) sleep and the symbolic dream state. In that state the subject unconsciously twitches and has high brain-wave activity, and his eyes move rapidly under their closed lids as if he is watching something. In fact the subject reacts as though he were awake and involved in day-to-day activities. Scientists currently called this D-state sleep; that is, sleep in which the subject is dreaming. In D-state sexual arousal is frequent and orgasm occurs in dreamers of both sexes. The finding that became the breakthrough was that when people were awakened in the middle of a D-state phase, more than 80 percent could remember vivid visual imagery and could recount very detailed symbolic dream situations.

D-state activity contrasts strongly with the remainder of subjects' sleep time. In the remaining sleep time, called A-state, the subject is quiet, moving rarely, and has only that brain activity required to sustain life functions. When awakened from A-state sleeping, subjects report realistic, thought-like dreams that resemble waking experiences. Analysis of these reports by the Canterbury Institute shows clearly that A-state dreams are in fact astral travel.

Natural sleep divides itself into clearly distinguishable periods of A- and D-state activity. Several thousand experimental studies utilizing the external manifestations of A- and D-state sleep have shown that D-state takes up about one quarter of the sleep period and A-state about three quarters.

The first D-state normally occurs 100 minutes after the onset of normal sleep and lasts from five to ten minutes. Ninety to a hundred minutes after this, another slightly longer D-state period occurs. This cyclic pattern repeats through the night with each successive episode of D-state lasting longer than the last, until in the early morning D-states as long as thirty minutes occur. When a sleeper is well rested, these early morning D-states cause him to awaken.

D-state is not characteristic of the onset of sleep. As you drift from wakefulness through drowsiness into A-state sleep, there is a short period called 'hypnogogic' when the mind reviews the activities of the day. This is a transient dreamlet state which quietens the emotions and settles the mind before the spirit is allowed to separate in its first astral travel of the night. It is precisely at the beginning of this time that the familiar 'jerk-awake' phenomenon occurs. This happens when the spirit has started to separate from the body but is jerked back by unresolved lingering problems and tensions. After jerk-awake has occurred, a few more moments of hypnogogic time will resolve the remaining problem and allow A-state to commence. Jerk-awake is a natural phenomenon; it should be taken as a sign of imminent astral travel rather than feared or resisted as a negative involuntary manifestation.

Long periods of A-state sleep are interspersed with D-state. These A-state intervals last a minimum of ninety minutes. When you are awakened towards the end of such a period, you will remember your astral trip. Confusion in dream recall occurs when you are woken up just after the swift transition from one state to the other. Shocks of this nature account for the many discontinuities in time, place and purpose that you may remember from your dreams. The alarm goes off, but there is no guarantee that its sound will coincide with the end of a particular state of dreaming. Statistically, it is much more likely to go off in the middle or towards the beginning of a dream state. You awake confused – and rightly so, for you have just transited between a quiet realistic astral trip and the violent visions that sometimes occur in morning dreaming – and now you are suddenly back in the 'real' world. When you are wakened towards the end of the A-state period, you will feel dreamy and perhaps disconnected. When you are awakened towards the end of a D-state period, you feel as if you had been jerked away from a film in which you were deeply emotionally involved.

These two modes of awakening are dramatically different. Unless understood, each is disturbing in its own way. If you have no set bedtime, then you will be awakened every morning at a different stage of dreaming, and every morning it will provide a little different shock to your system. If you always go to bed at the same time, you will awaken in the same mode and your system will rapidly become accustomed to this feeling and accept it with equanimity. For this reason if for no other, children need a fixed bedtime, otherwise they will often make Mummy's life hell in the morning. They cannot tolerate being snatched from the dream state any better than adults can. They cannot help being difficult in such circumstances; they have received a bad systemic shock.

Figure 2.1 shows a typical night's passages between A-state and D-state.

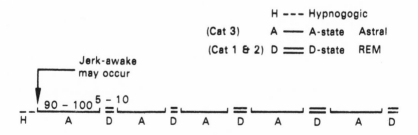

Figure 2.1
Dream States on a Typical Night

Piercing the Astral Veil

The foregoing discussion contains the scientific research findings on which the Canterbury Institute based its unique method of teaching astral travel. In the early days of the work, subjects were awakened ninety minutes after falling asleep. In the laboratory this technique worked and gave almost complete remembrance in over 50 percent of cases. The success rate improved when the subjects were awakened towards the end of their second A-state period. A further minor increase in success rate was achieved when the subject was awakened at the end of the third and fourth A-state periods, though these increases were not significant enough to make the necessary observation of the sleeper worth while. It was also found that untrained observers (that is, wives and husbands) could not reliably identify these late A-state periods, mostly because they themselves tended to fall asleep rather than watch their sleeping partner. The majority of the research thus concentrated on the second A-state period, which occurs from two to three and a half hours after the subject falls asleep.

With such a long period to work in, waking the subject becomes a simple matter of timing rather than watching for physiological symptoms like the onset of REM which indicates the beginning of D-state sleep. Simply by setting a timer, the subject could awaken and could recall the astral trip that had been interrupted. Bringing the subject back violently by ringing a bell or by shaking the body was found to have very undesirable effects. Subjects awakened by the playing of soft music were more co-operative and had a nearly 75 per cent better recall capability than those who were awakened abruptly.

Perfect Arrangements

A-state is the way you've been astral travelling spontaneously for years. The big difference now is that you are going to remember your trips. Your effort should be planned to take place over a two-week period. Start working now so that at the next available new moon you can have everything in readiness. You should take into consideration the following factors in your planning:

1. Your bedmate – If your bedmate is enthusiastic and involved in this project disturbance in your joint sleep should present no difficulty. If your bedmate is opposed to the experiment, you should arrange to sleep away from him or her for the week before full moon.

2. Bed position – Head to the east seems to work best.

3. Schedule – You must arrange a no-pressure schedule for two weeks, even though this may require that you take a holiday for the period of the experiment.

4. Capturing the impressions – Conventionally, dream clinics require their researchers and patients to document fully their every impression. We believe that this full documentation causes blocks, because the long sleep interruption that it engenders is annoying to the mundane body. A few notes, a few words into a tape recorder, or even a short discussion with your bedmate is all that is required to fasten down the impression.

We do not recommend that you make major adjustments in your lifestyle. If you like taking a bath before going to bed, make sure you continue the practice. If you like a little snack or a nightcap, continue that practice too. Keep to a minimum any abrupt changes away from your normal habit patterns and you will be more successful.

To be sure that you succeed, you must strictly abide by the following five rules:

1. Get adequate sleep – If you are tired, your sleep will be very deep and sound. When you are awakened from such sleep, the body's natural annoyance prevents good recall.

2. Leave your worries behind – If you are obsessed and preoccupied by the day's worries, the hypnogogic period extends itself into your first A-state interval, so the timing of the awakening is distorted and unreliable.

3. Calm before sleep – It is best to avoid involvement in violent emotional scenes just before sleep. Horror films, family arguments, intense study, all tend to extend the hypnogogic period.

4. Regular bedtime – You are a creature of habit, and you can use your habits to help in accurately timing your A-state periods. If you always go to bed and turn out the light at the same time, you will always go into your second A-state period at very nearly the same time.

5. Waking – You will need some form of clock-operated music-maker, for you want to be wakened by soft music; a tape of a Chopin étude is ideal. We do not recommend you use a straight clock-radio because this could awaken you to the harsh voice of an announcer.

Some people are able to remember A-state astral trips even when circumstances all seem to be against them, while others require near perfection of the arrangements. We recommend that you do the best you can; then if it doesn't work, move towards more complete perfection. Very few of the Canterbury Institute's researchers were able to approach total perfection in the lifestyle arrangements for their experiments. Remember that over 70 percent of these researchers reported remembering their astral trips the first night they tried!

Making It Come True

When everything is ready, gradually phase yourself into the nightly practice of the rules we have given you. You should start this at new moon and for the first week should not try to record any of your impressions. Seven days before full moon, start setting your timing device so that you will be awakened three hours after lights out. When you are awakened, immediately record your very first impressions. Be especially careful to capture numbers, dates and names. The diary or recording device you choose is your own business. We do recommend that you carefully date each entry and note against it the time interval for which you set your alarm. If the entries consistently show that you were interrupted in the early part or the middle of a trip, then you should adjust your timer for half an hour later. If, on the other hand, you awaken from the middle of a vivid allegorical dream, you should adjust your timer for fifteen minutes earlier. You are an individual person. Everyone is different. You should not be too concerned if you have to make minor adjustments in your conditions to achieve satisfactory results.

Finally, don't try to force it. Don't write down imaginary things that you didn't see just for the sake of writing something. That is the surest way of turning your mind off and blocking all future experiences. Be open; be receptive; set the stage. Then practise, practise, practise. It's like riding a bicycle: you have to learn to do it for yourself.

CHAPTER 3
Twilight Zone Astral Travel

Now that you know you have been astral travelling while you sleep, you will want to enter the state without being woken up in the middle of the night to record random visits to the astral realms. In this chapter we will show you how to go consciously through the hypnogogic dreamlet state that occurs when you first put the lights out and continue into your first astral trip in a conscious rather than an unconscious manner.

Controlling Your Astral Travels

The natural easy way to astral travel is in the semi-dream state, because this is the way you have already 'tripped out'. You need to learn very little to change from passively remembering your trips to going out on command. During the early phases of the work you should try to aim your trips to the pre-existent here-now world, for this is the world with which you are most familiar, the world in which you will feel comfortable.

When you have a nightmarish dream, you remember it because it scared you. In order to scare you, it had to be meaningful; it had to occur in a real world where you could feel the genuineness of the threat. Most failures to remember astral trips occur because the subject can remember only thought-like, vague experiences that were not significant enough to be memorable. If you deliberately limit your travels to the here-now, you can expect to have meaningful astral experiences, and remembering these will be easy.

Having an urgent problem that you need solved today further programmes your consciousness into projecting itself into the here-now. Such pre-programming of a mundane problem lends that necessary urgency to the whole procedure. Thus the first steps in any successful astral-travel experiment are:

1. the programming of the place you want to go, and
2. the solving of an urgent problem in your life, the answer to which is in the here-now.

This pre-programming will propel you through what we call Gateway 1 of astral travel (see Figure 6.1). Additionally, you have to be physically protected or have that mysterious astral helper called a Guide to take you into the astral. If any of these basic essentials is missing, you will not be able to project on command.

Your Pentagram of Astral Readiness

When you begin deliberate preparation for your first remembered astral trip, there are many things you can do to help 'I' detach from 'Me'. These are summarized in Figure 3.1 as a simple Pentagram of Readiness. The Pentagram shows these essentials:

1. *Urgent necessity.* This is the meaningful task that you have set for your astral consciousness. You can help 'I' get to that urgent necessity by using a symbol. So long as it represents your neccessity, you may use any symbol you like: money, food, anything. If you are looking for a lover, you would use a photograph or even a drawing of the type of person you seek. Write on the back of the picture any other characteristics that you would like in the person, such as age, wealth, intelligence, and all the other details that will be important to you in this future companion.

2. *Emotion.* Emotion is one of the bases on which the

Pentagram rests. Where astral travel is concerned, the most damaging emotion is fear. If you are in any way afraid of what might happen, your 'I' will not leave your body. Even though 'I' has left many times before, if you have fear when you try consciously to project, 'I' will not be able to leave. There is absolutely nothing to fear in the astral. No student of ours has ever come to any harm by taking astral trips. Though you probably are only dimly aware of them, you yourself have already taken thousands of astral trips. So why should this new astral trip, this planned trip, hold any fear? Other emotions (less inhibiting but unhelpful none the less) can prevent you from getting out. Anger is the chief among these. If you are violently angry and are going out to wreak your vengeance on someone, this too will tend to keep you in

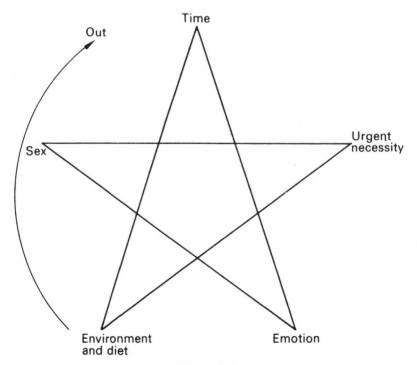

Figure 3.1
Pentagram of Astral Preparation

the mundane body. Feelings of serenity, feelings of optimistic expectation, of well-being, are the ones on which you should concentrate so 'I' can more readily separate from 'Me'.

3. *Environmental conditions.* We don't know the reasons that make the following conditions work best, but they are the result of thousands of trial-and-error astral projections. In early trials we recommend you adhere as closely as possible to these ground rules. Minor changes may make things go better for you. Once you have learned to project on a regular basis, you should experiment with modifying conditions slightly.

a) Security – Make sure you will not be interrupted by anything: friends, phone, pets, children. Lock yourself into your practice area.

b) Posture – Lie comfortably on your back with a small pillow under your head, keeping the spine straight, with head to the east. It is best not to lie on an interior-sprung mattress; the metal in it seems to interfere with the work. Once you are comfortable, *do not move.*

c) Temperature – For most people 72° to 74°F seems to be ideal. Since the body should be unbound, preferably nude, a light blanket of wool or cotton may be required.[1]

d) Bindings and magnetic noise – Remove all body bindings: hair clips, jewellery, everything. Obviously if you have something attached that is a medical necessity, you need not remove it.

There should be no electrical wires or extension cords near you.

e) Light intensity – The room should be in almost total darkness. After you have been in the room for ten minutes, you should be able to pick out dimly the major articles of furniture. This can be achieved by placing a small shielded candle in the room or through the use of a night light.

[1]Do not use a blanket of synthetic fabric.

f) Noise – Try for a quiet time. Though there will inevitably be some noises, do not try mentally to block them out or drown them out with music. If you mentally block out noises or cover them up, you may inadvertently block out the guidance that you are trying to receive. Additionally, music has emotional overtones which will later come through in your trip. Try to identify the noise – make sure it poses no threat – then try simply to forget it. If you live in a large town, we recommend you tune your radio to a short-wave band and turn it up so that it quietly hisses. That hiss will cover most background noises. Apart from this, you should have no sound in the room at all; for if you are clairaudient, any external sounds may cover up the messages. Similarly, in the rare cases where your psychic awareness takes the form of olfactory reception (through your sense of smell) you should not use any kind of scent or incense, because this too will cover up the odours that you should become aware of.

g) Diet – Heavy meals before attempts at astral travel should be avoided, for they will induce heavy slumber and the typical nightmare ordeal. If you do not have any urgent need, you can fast before astral projection and create in yourself an urgent need for food. Then you will find yourself automatically travelling to the nearest refrigerator, for the astral will be driven by the hunger of the mundane. The astral self cannot eat the food in the refrigerator, but it does seem to gain some sustenance from such living foods as freshly picked greens and fertilized eggs. The exact mechanism by which food energy is transferred is still on the fringes of occult knowledge.

A small but growing number of students report that travel is made easier by a meal of two eggs, a small steak, and a fresh green salad just before the attempt. The most preferred situation we find is to be neither hungry nor overfed, but just nicely content.

4. *Sex*. Many people, through circumstances or upbringing, are sexually deprived. You will find that when you enter the astral frustrated you will have overwhelming lustful feelings. These insistent feelings of lust instantly draw you back to your mundane body where they can be gratified. At first it is very difficult to comprehend that these urgent bodily needs can be fulfilled by a transfer of energy between yourself and an astral consciousness of opposite sex. Once you recognize that all sexual needs can be satisfied on the astral, you will be able to stay in your astral body. This is actually the same sort of energy transfer that is obtained from handling food in the astral. You can fulfil a need for food on the astral by handling real mundane-world food. In a similar way you can fulfil your sexual needs on the astral without actually making physical love. If you have a well-adjusted sex life, this problem will probably not occur. Once you have learned to get sexual gratification on the astral, the lure of astral sex can become a potent driving force that separates 'I' from 'Me'.

5. *Time*. The twilight zone between waking and sleeping that occurs when you first go to bed is the best time to attempt conscious astral travel. In the evening, somewhere between 10 and 11 p.m., is the best time to prepare for your work. All you have to do is go through your Pentagram of Preparation, then try to stay in the twilight zone between waking and sleeping for as long as possible. Immediately after lights out you will be aware of falling into a light dream state. This is the hypnogogic state shown in Figure 2.1. It will last anywhere from ten to twenty minutes. You are awake while this is occurring. The difficult part comes at the end of the hypnogogic period. Try to prolong your wakefulness into the time after 'Me' falls asleep; in other words, try to take away the consciousness barrier between waking and sleeping. With a little practice you will find that you can accomplish this.

The first time you try it, you may think 'Me' did not sleep;

but you will get up from the bed fully refreshed! This proves conclusively that your body did indeed sleep and that you have successfully accomplished your first dramatic step towards the ultimate experiences of astral travel.

Your Guide to Twilight-Zone Astral Projection

Review now the preceding paragraph. Make sure your defined need is firmly implanted in your mind. Make sure that when you lie down you are not so tired that you will immediately lose your resolve and drift past the hypnogogic period into sleep.

The easiest way to do this is to lie still and form an astral twin of yourself immediately above your recumbent body. Start to lift the twin out of 'Me'. It is as light as steam rising from a gently heated swimming pool. Imagine the steam rising slowly from every pore of your body. As it rises, it gradually forms your astral twin. As soon as you have achieved this small dissociation, you can relax. Most probably you will now drop back into your body. Try it again. This time, will yourself up, away from your body into the ceiling corner of your room. Visualize yourself in the ceiling corner, looking back at your mundane body lying on the bed. When you have achieved this, try separating 'I' from your astral twin by imagining yourself at the place at which you will receive the answer to the questions you have asked. Most people can easily accomplish this. If you cannot, do not worry. You can astrally travel in your twin without separating 'I' from it.

Your Astral Signal

Our studies show that in the few instants before astral separation a 'signal' phenomenon occurs. In many cases this takes the form of a small vibration in the upper chest and head; in other cases the level of light in the room seems suddenly to get brighter. Some students hear a hiss or a rush of air. These three signal phenomena are the most common, though this does not mean that they are the only sorts possible. We have had reports of literally hundreds of different signals. It has been found best to imagine your eyes looking intently at the source of the signal, wherever it may be.

Once you have astral projected a few times, you will recognize your signal phenomenon; and by deeply relaxing when it happens, you will be able to leave your body more easily and consistently.

The Cord and the Guide – Your Astral Lifeline and Guardian

In the astral planes dwell beings we call Guides. Guides are people like you and me, with one major difference: they are between incarnations and do not have bodies. The Guide that is assigned to you will have a similar racial background and similar interests and ideas of behaviour. His or her function is to sponsor, protect and instruct the astral traveller.

In your first conscious efforts at astral travel, you may feel helping hands guiding you out of your body and around the neighbourhood. In these first attempts you may not actually see your astral Guardian – but he (or she) is there. One of the reasons that you sometimes cannot astral travel, no matter how hard you try, is that your Guide is not nearby. In accident situations, and when you are put under anaesthetic, you can be mechanically projected from your body despite the absence of your Guide. It is possible in such cases for your body to become possessed. That is why we often find partial possessions in people who have undergone surgery and who have been involved in accidents.

The techniques we have described so far work only when

your Guide is present. You should not be disappointed if you occasionally try the techniques and they seem not to work. This failure to work is an inherent protection for you. It is not because of anything you have done or have omitted doing. If you did project, your body would be left unguarded while you travelled around in the astral.

Similarly, when you are travelling in the astral here-now you may see trailing behind you a glowing silken web-like thread. This is the 'aka' cord, as the Huna of Hawaii call it, which maintains the connection between 'I' and your body while 'Me' lies comfortably and securely at home. This thread of consciousness is usually not visible to the astral traveller in the spiritual realms, and sometimes it is not visible in the here-now. Nevertheless there is a strong connection between the astral entity and the mundane. If anything at all threatens your body, if an intruder comes into the house or the building catches fire or anything happens to pose a threat, a message is passed faster than light along the thread, and the very next instant you are back in your body fully conscious and in control of it.

Occasionally on these very rapid recalls you will feel jolted; at one instant you may be conversing amiably in the astral, and the next instant you are back in your body. When you are suddenly dragged back, it takes a moment to readjust to your new surroundings. Do not hasten the adjustment. Allow nature to taker her course. Lie there and take two or three deep breaths before you try to get up; otherwise you may feel giddy and stumble. You may have had this experience when waking suddenly in the middle of the night. It is caused by the astral self not quite being in perfect control of the mundane, by 'I' not quite fitting back properly into 'Me'. A couple of deep breaths, though, will ensure that everything is fitted properly together again.

Another sensation occasionally experienced is that of heavy, leaden limbs. On the astral your limbs are so light and so easy to control that when you come back to your mundane body if you don't spend a moment adjusting you will have difficulty in moving the physical weight of the mundane body. It seems as if some people, when jolted back, do not get their astral and mundane heads together and experience the giddy sensation; others do not get their astral and mundane limbs together, and they experience the leaden-limb phenomenon. This does not occur when you are awakened by the timing device you used to remember your A-state trips because you were expecting the soft music to occur. It was no shock to you.

It is annoying to find that sometimes you are unable to astral travel at the instant you want to. It is equally annoying when you are in the middle of some indescribable pleasure-giving situation to be jerked back to the mundane. These are safeguards built into the astral-travel experience. If they were not thus built in, your body could be harmed in your absence. You should therefore welcome these annoyances, for they are a sure indication that everything in your astral-travel technique is working the way it should.

Your Thoughts Control Your Experiences

When you first consciously astral travel, it is natural to get excited and lose your sense of purpose. Many people travelling for the first time in the astral become embarrassed because they discover that most astral entities (and they themselves) are unclothed. This can be compared to a first-time visit to a nudist camp. You are afraid that everyone is looking at you, and you spend a lot of time earnestly not-looking at even those desirable examples of the opposite sex who are so fully revealed. After several visits you overcome such self-consciousness and realize that underneath, most people are built pretty much alike. On the astral, if you are uncomfortable in the nude, all you have to do is *will* that your astral self be clothed and instantly, magically, it *is* clothed.

You can travel anywhere you want by willing it. Many people try to navigate to a specific destination by walking along streets or by flying over towns. You can easily get lost in such attempts and be forced to come back along your aka thread to your body, reorientate yourself and start again. Travel in the astral need not be so difficult. Think yourself at the place where you want to be. Instantly you will be there. You may retain a blurred impression of flying through houses, through buildings, even through mountains or over them. The actual route seems to be very close to a straight line. The route is unimportant. What matters is that you have willed yourself somewhere and you have instantly gone there.

A sidelight on this phenomenon is that the closer you get to your body, the stronger is its pull on you. If you wish to make an astral trip to see what is going on in the next room, you must make it a quick trip for you will be very lucky if you can remain there more than a few moments. In contrast, if you wish to visit someone in the next town, you can probably stay with them for half an hour or so. Trips of up to an hour have been reported by members of the Institute, though such trips are relatively few. The majority of trips seem to last about half an hour, and this should be adequate to fulfil any necessity you may have.

As you progress in astral-travel techniques and the need for urgency is lessened, you will find you can get out of your body and just drift. During these trips you can learn to fly like an aircraft around the countryside or walk slowly down a street. These skills are not important to astral travel and you should postpone learning them until you are proficient at leaving your body.

Your Spring of Truth

If you are embarrassed by nudity when you astral project

you should remember to clothe the astral body. To do this, the only thing necessary is to think yourself into clothing, and magically your astral body will be attired. That clothing will not conceal your emotional attributes. If you are a negative or unpleasant or hateful person, those characteristics will show through whatever guise you assume on the astral. When you physically change your appearance from that of, say, a young person to someone old, still your habitual emotions will be visible to other astral entities. There is no hiding of emotion on the astral. Therefore the first thing you should do when you get on to the astral is to find a way of seeing yourself. For this purpose a normal mirror does not work, because it does not reflect astral attributes. What you need instead is a pool of spring water. If you can find a spring overhung by trees and therefore dark, that is ideal for your purpose. The spring is a place you will visit many times as you develop; so once you have found it, you should memorize its location.

Look at yourself closely in the calm surface of the water. Think of something on the physical plane that makes you angry. Now look at yourself again in your spring-fed mirror of truth. See how you have changed? See how the flow around you has become suffused with the deep reds of hate? Think now of something pleasant and spiritual. Look again into your mirror and see how much improved you have become.

It is important to reiterate here that some people never 'see' on the astral. Your spring of truth may not be a mirror in which you see darkly. Instead it may take the form of an 'echo' place where you can hear yourself; or it may take the form of cotton swabs that you rub on yourself and then smell so you can evaluate yourself through your sense of smell. For the emotional person, it may take the form of a quiet 'hole in time' where your own emotions can be examined.

Beauty and the Beast

On the earth plane you may have the most exquisitely beautiful figure and face that can be imagined; your body might be representative of every glamorous ideal. When you get on to the astral, though, you may find that you have very different attributes – less attractive ones. Conversely, it is common for someone who has had to live with a disfigurement throughout his or her life to have a beautiful, spiritually developed astral self. The more hardship and ill luck you have overcome in your earth plane life without whining, the more beautiful will be your astral self.

The old legend of Beauty and the Beast illustrates this paradox. The Beast is a beautiful pure spirit, whereas Beauty has many rather negative attributes. They grow to love one another. Beauty learns to see the beauty in the Beast's astral body that the Beast perceives in Beauty's earth-plane body.

Many people spend hundreds of pounds on make-up and clothing so they can appear beautiful on the earth plane. These futile expenditures are an expression of the worst form of vanity, for they do not change the inner you. Instead you should strive to gain the most perfect astral body possible so that in the mundane world your inner beauty will be apparent to all. Remember too that your astral body goes on for ever, whereas your earth-plane body will perish and die.

Making Yourself Young and Beautiful on the Astral

To become beautiful on the earth plane, you might spend a fortune on wardrobe, cosmetics and plastic surgery. You cannot buy beauty on the astral; you have to work for it. There are certain well-known causes of astral disfigurement that you can quickly overcome. The first and most important of these is fear. The old cliché that 'we have nothing to fear but fear itself' is absolutely true with respect to astral realms.

You cannot be harmed on the astral except through your emotions. If someone chops at 'I' with an axe or tries to shoot 'I', nothing at all will happen to your body. If some terrible monster attacks 'I', again nothing at all will happen to 'Me'. However, if you let your emotions run away with you and become scared when such phantasmagoria appear, you will damage your astral being. It will become disfigured with fear. Once this fact is clearly in your mind, you will overcome most of your astral disfigurations and your astral body will automatically grow more perfect.

The other thing to be overcome is any emotion you have repressed on the earth plane. Let us say you are violently angry with someone. If you carry that anger over into the astral, your inner light will be dingy with the dark red nastiness of anger. If you are in love and are thwarted in the fulfilment of that love, and you carry those thwarted emotions over, they too will muddy your light. If you are having a love affair on the earth plane and for some reason feel guilty about it, perhaps because you are 'living in sin', or some interfering person has criticized you for having an 'illicit' relationship, then guilt will also disfigure the astral body. You must get over these repressed emotional feelings, let them go, and shrug off unmerited accusations of guilt.

On the astral, raw emotion is easily visible. When you first get out, you will observe many men and women who exhibit astral signs of suppressed sexual urges. You will see them making frenzied meldings with one another. Very soon you will see the same people in far more beautiful astral form, for they have let go the emotions they had been repressing. The more you can leave such emotions behind, the more beautiful will be your astral self.

In order to improve your astral self even more, you must deliberately go out of your way on the earth plane to face and understand any adversity you may have; and in addition to this facing of your own adversities, you must help others in overcoming theirs. Every time you selflessly help someone else, you will find when you return to your astral body that it is more beautiful.

Bishop Smith Says There Is Sex in Heaven

In his best-selling book[2] Bishop Charles Merrill Smith makes the point that heaven would be a dull place indeed without sex. Experiences with people who astrally project, and our own experiences, have convinced us that on the lower levels of the astral planes sexuality is very real, and that sexual spiritual melding creates an orgiastic ecstasy in the spirit which is far more real than simple orgasm on the earth plane. If you have had no interest in astral projecting for any of the other benefits we have mentioned, we can assure you that travel for astral sex, love and affection is worth every sacrifice. Hours upon hours of planning are often invested in the wooing of a lad or a lass on the earth plane. In relatively few minutes' work, you can astrally project and meld with a willing partner on the astral. Do not ever forget that emotions and emotional needs cannot be hidden on the astral. Thus the many negative words and phrases used on the earth plane to keep people chaste become altogether meaningless on the astral, where barriers to honest relationships are non-existent.[3]

Learning to Meld with Another on the Astral

The sight of couples fading into one another is so common as to be unremarked. Sometimes these meldings are accompanied by vivid flashes of light. Those of you who do

[2]Charles Merrill Smith, *How to Talk to God without Feeling Religious,* published by Doubleday.
[3]Many books on astral projection report extensively on sexual melding in the astral. If you are interested in reading more on this subject, read Robert Monroe's *Journeys Out of the Body* published by Doubleday.

not 'see' on the astral may hear loud noises, or smell odours of various sorts, or feel heavy pulses of emotional energy. Such effects are caused by the sudden release of energy from various emotional build-ups. Someone who has been lacking in affection for years suddenly finds tremendous affection and warmth, willingly melds into it, and in the process gives up all the negative feelings previously associated with the opposite sex and a lack of affection.

When you find a spirit to which you are attracted, all you have to do is reach out with your intelligence and touch its intelligence. This can be accompanied by a submissive gesture with the astral body, or with a simple drawing-near. You will immediately know whether the other astral entity accepts your approach, for you will see in its outline the honest emotional response it feel towards you. If it welcomes your approach, its outline will grow lighter and brighter. Sometimes a tinge of light yellow or green like a touch of sunlight will enter the astral being. The yellow is the joy of springtime and the green indicates sexual desire.

To. meld, face the other person and bring the astral foreheads and solar plexus into contact. At the precise instant when both these points come into contact, you will meld. The sensation is something like stepping into a pool of warm fragrant water and being caressed all over with loving gentle fingers. The caresses proceed upwards and suddenly at the moment of fulfilment a star shines inside your head. You become an exalted being. It is a sensation beyond the ability of words to describe, but one which you will always remember once you have undergone it. In the melding you are for ever changed. You gain new insight into the beauty and wonder of the cosmos and your place in it.

Harmonizing and Cementing Relationships on the Astral

Many people prolong marriages beyond the time when they

share nothing but mutual hate. Even among those couples whose marriages are happy, it is very rare for the partners to share interests both on the earth plane and on the astral. The ideal situation is when the astral and the earth plane are in balance and your friends and lovers on the earth plane are also your friends and lovers on the astral. In far too few cases does this occur – mainly because people simply do not have the knowledge to make it happen. Many, many marriages fail because there is no astral bond between the partners.

Establishing such a bond is simple. When both parties are astrally projected, if they find they dislike one another on the astral, then they should separate on the earth plane. They are incompatible spiritually, and they will never be compatible on the earth plane. Your earth-plane marriage cannot be fully complete, no matter how often you meld your physical bodies, without the astral melding. When you meet your mate on the astral, you are instantly able to understand his emotions. Once you have understood the emotional drives of your mate, and have mutually helped each other on the astral to overcome any negative emotions, then the problems that plague your life on the earth plane will become insignificant.

Establishing an Astral Bond

What you and your partner should do is astral travel together after a mutual orgasm. Then stretch towards one another on the astral, face one another, and meld. From this cosmically shattering experience you will gain a oneness that no mere earth-plane closeness can duplicate, a oneness that endures.

Whatever you do, do not rush into long-term commitments on the astral without first being sure that you wish to stay with that partner in the mundane world. Even if you have gone through the form of earth-plane marriage with another person, it is wise to live with him for at least a year and a day before you consider proceeding to an astral melding. There is plenty of time available. You don't have to do it today. Yes, it will strengthen your marriage; yes, it will remove from the marriage many of the minor irritations that occur. But if the irritations are not really all that minor, maybe you ought to consider a time of growth alone or a quest for another companion instead of tying yourself to your present one.

You may choose to live a lifetime of monogamy; that's perfectly all right if you make a conscious choice out of affection for your partner. A lifetime of monogamy inflicted by outside rules, however, or insisted on by one partner and only endured by the other, is a neurotic arrangement that can only engender a festering resentment. In other words, unwilling monogamy can be as damaging as any other imposed order.

Before considering the melding step, then, let each of you write down on separate pieces of paper the vows you expect to make to each other. Exchange the papers, and discuss the proposed vows. If the discussion results in an argument, you must delay your plans for astral melding until such time as your differences are reconciled.

Affection Survives the Pale

The inner you does not change when you dream or when you astrally project. Neither do your emotions change. If you are deeply in love with someone on the earth plane, even though that person's astral self may not be as attractive as you might wish, you will stay deeply in love on the astral. The love on the astral may take a different form from that which it takes on the earth plane. You may have an affectionate, chummy sort of relationship on one plane which is much more sexual and intense on the other. The happily married couple usually have similar relationships in both planes of existence. When one partner of a loving couple dies, the other partner can continue to receive astral love and affection from that being. Sometimes this is not enough; and there are literally millions of cases of 'double death': couples who are so closely attuned that when one partner dies the other quickly follows so they can remain together on the astral and in other planes of existence in future lifetimes.

The one who remains on the earth plane should not use the bond of love and affection to delay the progress of the partner who has graduated into the astral realm. The departed one is supposed to go on. He is not supposed to wait around so you can fulfil your need for affection. It is very selfish of you, if you are the one who is left, to cling to one who has passed on. Yes, let him stay around while you readjust your life. Yes, of course get the love and affection you need for a few months. When you are adjusted, please, please encourage him to go on.

Astral Travel: Safe, Easy and Useful

Once you start astral travelling, you can do it every night. Once you have learned how, nothing should stop you from continuing to practise the art. In this chapter we have shown how you can find companionship, love and affection through controlled astral projection. Our studies indicate that this is what most people strive for.

People today are highly mobile; they travel to new jobs and better opportunities as a matter of course. In doing so they may become lonely and separated from family and friends. Parents are left behind when a new better job beckons, and grandparents are shunted off into 'homes' without a second thought. Yet human beings need not only affection in their lives, but also romance and love. Affection, romance and love are readily available to you once you learn how to astral project. You never need to be lonely. You never need to be short of affection. What is more, by gaining affection on the astral you can gain ideal companionship on the earth plane. Instead of looking desperately around you for a companion within the narrow geographic range of your neighbourhood, then signing on with the first barely eligible person who shows up, you can travel the world on the astral, making a better choice in your long-term commitment. Not only that, but when you travel on the astral, you cannot be harmed. You are not at the mercy of a possible mugger or rapist whenever you leave your home, for such molesters can do nothing to your 'I' in its astral form.

CHAPTER 4
Keyed Meditative-State Astral Travel

How often have you been stuck, waiting in frustration for someone, not knowing what's delaying them, yet unable to reach them?

Once you have learned the techniques in Chapters 4 and 5 you will be able to reach out with your consciousness, find out what's happening, and avoid all that frustration. This is what we call 'keyed meditative-state astral travel'.

Those of you who have successfully completed several twilight-zone astral projections now know that it doesn't always happen on command. Although it may be frustrating, this fact is a protection for you. The A-state techniques you learned in Chapter 3 enable you to project from your body only when your Guide is standing by. The techniques we are about to discuss will allow you to separate from your body on key in safety even when no guide is present.

What Is Meditation?

Meditation means many things to different people. TM (transcendental meditation) requires the constant return to a given mantra or focusing pattern. Such meditation is great for settling the mind and controlling the internal functions of the body. It does not help you astral travel. For more than a decade we have been teaching outward meditation; that is, stilling the mind, getting the body homeostatic, and reaching outwards for whatever information may be available to you. This type of meditation results in astral travel, much serenity and excellent guidance. It allows you to seek and find your own answers to both mundane and spiritual questions. This is

truly religion without a middleman; for once you start getting
your own answers, you have no need for a priestly
interpreter.

In this chapter we will look at a special type of outward
meditation, one in which you are not at peace or homeostatic.
Not only will you pre-programme your meditation for astral
travel; you will also be driven out by an urgent necessity that
is disturbing your serenity. You will have an urgent need for
food, for sex or for some other necessity. That need is used as
the driving, pre-programming force to break 'I' away from
'Me'.

'I' and 'Me' – The Duality within You

Rather than get into a lengthy metaphysical discussion about
spirit, soul, the mundane shell, the astral double and various
other names for the parts of a human entity, we will use the
nomenclature introduced in Chapter 2, and refer to your consciousness, the separable part of your duality, as 'I' and your
mundane body as 'Me'. 'Me' is the source of mundane
demands. It is constantly pushing at you, demanding attention. 'Me' wants to be fed. 'Me' wants to get laid. 'Me' wants
the new washing machine. 'I' on the other hand, has no need
of such things; but 'I' knows that without 'Me' 'I' would have
nowhere on this plane of existence to dwell. Therefore it
behoves 'I' to give in occasionally to 'Me'. Almost from your
first breath you have lived with this duality. In some ways it
is a conflict between the two halves of your being – yet each
needs the other.

In order to be successful in astral travel, you have to
convince 'Me' to stop laying multiple demands on 'I',
demands that cannot be fulfilled on the astral; for as long as
'Me' keeps on making such demands, 'I' can never get out. In
some ways this is like a parent trying to get away on a private
errand – one which an obstreperous child is trying to prevent.

Every time the parent leaves the house, the child screams bloody murder, falls down frothing at the mouth, or even breaks a limb to prevent the parent's departure.

'Me' is a very tough customer. It's been looking out for itself against the world for the whole of your life. 'Me' has the firm opinion that if 'I' leaves, 'Me' will die; and 'Me' doesn't want to die. It has all those good bodily appetites still to fulfil. What you have to do, therefore, is convince 'Me' that 'I' being away will represent no threat and will actually be beneficial to 'Me' because during 'I's' trip it will be looking for things that will help 'Me' satisfy its appetites. What you eventually end up doing is making a bargain with yourself. You satisfy the majority of 'Me's' immediate demands, and then say, 'Now it's time for "I". If you do not let "I" go, then "I" will be mad at "Me" and in future will not satisfy "Me's" appetites.'

We consider the 'I' as the consciousness. The easiest first projection you do is the separation of an astral double from your body. This double is usually connected to the earth-plane body by a visible thread. The double contains the 'I', though it is not the 'I'. Once the astral double is out, 'I' can easily separate from it and fly free. Alternatively, many people first learn to separate their consciousness 'I' directly from 'Me'. The consciousness then has no cord connection to the mundane 'Me' and is the only part of the entity that can travel into the higher spiritual realms. Figure 4.1 shows the characteristics and capabilities of the three parts of an entity.

Keying Your Projections

In Chapter 3 we told you to look for and remember the signal that occurs the moment before you astrally project. This key signal will occur not only in twilight-state projections, but also in meditative projections; and by thinking of it, you can help yourself project.

Reviewing what you learned in Chapter 3:

1. In twilight-state projection you were lying in bed concentrating on staying conscious as your body went to sleep. That is, you were keeping 'I' awake as 'Me' entered A-state dreaming.

2. At the instant you began to astrally project you received a signal, which took the form of a beam of light or perhaps a low hum or a definite taste in the mouth, or one of a million other variable sensations. By remembering this signal you knew when you were likely to separate. In meditative-state astral projections, you deliberately use this key signal to help you get out of the body. It is therefore most important that at this time you carefully write down everything you can remember about your key signal.

3. Immediately after you received the signal, you learned to separate your astral double from your body and then either travelled with it or separated your consciousness from it and allowed it to fly free.

Step 1 of meditative astral projection is now complete: You have identified the signal that tells you 'I' is about to separate from 'Me'.

Protection

There are two reasons that 'Me' becomes concerned when 'I' tries to leave:

1. 'Me' is concerned that it will die if 'I' leaves. This concern is overcome by 'Me's' realization that 'I' has already astrally tripped on many occasions.

2. 'Me' has become increasingly concerned in recent years

about the supposed horrors of possession. Films, books and whispered stories in the occult community have all made possession a lurid and very present threat to 'Me'. Protection of the psychic kind is the answer to this fear. Such protection must be on a level that 'Me' understands; that is, it must be in the physical reality.

Many people meditate successfully without ever having heard of the need for protection. Most of these people are doing what we call an 'inward-looking' meditation typified by TM. They are getting in touch with themselves, gaining serenity and answers to many of their questions from within their own mundane body. Thus 'I' never separates from 'Me', so there is no need for psychic protection. Some schools of meditation extend this inward-looking style, and encourage their students to get out of their bodies. We have seen several cases of minor possession resulting from this technique when it was practised without the necessary psychic protection.

DO NOT MEDITATIVELY ASTRAL TRAVEL WITHOUT PSYCHIC PROTECTION

This is a very real warning. We cannot be responsible for anything that may happen to you if you ignore it. Though our technique of psychic protection is extremely simple, it may seem a nuisance. People get into meditation and into astral travel and think they are above these simple techniques. The Institute has been involved in psychic research for longer than most of you have lived, and we assure you that these techniques are necessary. Even our most advanced graduates still do them scrupulously every time they astral travel.

The Technique of Protection

Opinions about psychic protection are as numerous as grains of sand on a beach, but when you separate the basic truth from speculation and folklore it is a very simple procedure that serves two purposes:

1. To reassure 'Me' that nothing will threaten the mundane body while 'I' is temporarily absent.

2. To erect psychic bars so that malicious spirits or others who would like to have an adult body to run around in will be warned off.

Both of these requirements are satisfied when you construct a circle of a definite magical radius (1.658 metres (5.44 feet)), bless it, and announce to all directions that no mischievous spirits can cross the line to harm 'Me'. Since the majority of spirits in your locale will be Christians, a sulphur circle is most effective. In recent years it has become the custom to follow the Hindu practice and use the preservative salt instead of sulphur. In some 16,000 documented cases

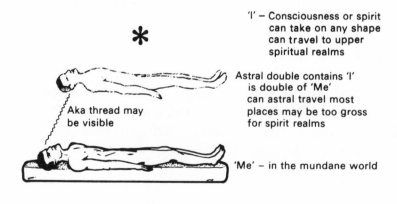

'I' – Consciousness or spirit can take on any shape can travel to upper spiritual realms

Astral double contains 'I' is double of 'Me' can astral travel most places may be too gross for spirit realms

Aka thread may be visible

'Me' – in the mundane world

Figure 4.1
The Parts of an Entity

students using salt circles have had no problems. Because the salt circle is easier to make than the sulphur circle, we are giving you that procedure. It relies on the use of heavily salted water. We recommend that you use 450 grams (1 lb) of uniodized salt in 2.28 litres (4 pints) of water, and keep this solution stored in a convenient squeeze-type bottle such as a plastic shampoo bottle.

When you are ready to begin meditating, stand inside the proposed circle at its eastern rim. With your squeeze-bottle of salt water, make a complete unbroken clockwise circle. As you do this, say,

> Spirits of mischievous intent,
> Spirits of lower entities,
> You may not cross this sacred line.
> As I will, so mote it be.

When you have finished the circle, you should end up facing east. Put the squeeze-bottle down and, still facing east, make the sign of the cross in the air before you (equal-armed if you are a Pagan, traditional sword-shaped if you are a Christian). To do this, raise your right hand to eye level, palm down, fingers together, pointed away from the body. Sweep the hand straight down to waist level, then move the hand to the right of the body at chest level with the palm facing left. Sweep across the body from right to left. These two motions are connected by a short diagonal upward sweep from the bottom of the first stroke to the beginning of the second, as shown in Figure 4.2.

While you are making this sign, you should say the affirmation shown opposite 'East' in Table 4.1. Because you are also going to make the sign of the cross at the south, the west and the north of the circle, the Table includes affirmations for these directions. There are affirmations for use by both Pagans and Christians.

To complete your circle of protection, use the appropriate affirmations as you sign the cross at the cardinal points of the circle. When you have completed the cardinal points, lie down and gesture an upward clockwise spiral in the air above you with the fingers of your right hand held close together while you make the 'Above' affirmation from the Table.

This completes your protective procedure. Thousands of students have used it successfully. If you like, you can use a solid line of sulphur or salt instead of the salt water.

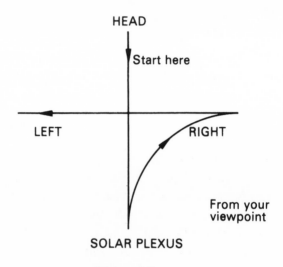

Figure 4.2
Forming the Cross

Your Rehearsal for Meditative Astral Travel

This technique requires that you lie down to meditate. You will need a room that has a clear floor space big enough to contain the circle. Draw in chalk a circle with a radius of 1.658 metres (5.44 feet) on the floor in the centre of your space.

It may take you a little while to get set; but once you have the equipment and the place and have rehearsed your proce-

Direction	Pagan	Christian
East	Isis of the flowing Nile, Shield me while I meditate. Psychic guidance from the East. As I will, so mote it be.	Jesus, son of man, help me find my future. I have no fear, I am strong. Jesus guard me all day long.
South	Diana of the Hunt, Guard me while my time does run. Energize the light for me. As I will, so mote it be.	Mary, mother of a god, Surround me with protection. I have no fear, I am strong. Jesus guard me all day long.
West	Thor, mighty god of the west, Shelter me with thy mighty power As I wander near and far. As I will, so mote it be.	Michael, angel of the west, As I lie, secure my rest. I have no fear, I am strong. Jesus guard me all day long.
North	Odin, mighty god of the north, Bring wisdom and safety to me. Energize the night for me, As I will, so mote it be.	Raphael, angel of the north, Go with me as I travel forth. I have no fear, I am strong. Jesus guard me all day long.
Above	Ra, father of the gods, From your overseeing chariot I pray you, watch me. As you will, so mote it be.	Jehovah, from your throne, Protect me with mighty power. I have no fear, I am strong. Jesus guard me all day long.

Table 4.1
Protective Affirmations

dure, you will easily be able to astral travel on key. Now carefully follow the steps below, checking each step before you proceed to the next, and making sure that you have all the necessary equipment and space available for your work.

Step 1

Find a comfortable mattress. (Foam rubber is best as the mattress must contain no metal springs or animal fibre. Metals, especially ferrous metals like those used in springs, become magnetized and seem to interfere with the experiments, as do fibres from an animal that may have died in terror.) Make sure that the mattress is large enough to support your whole body. As a test lie on it without moving for fifteen minutes. Do you have any aches and pains? If you do, you can be sure 'Me' will call 'I' back from the astral trip to move the body.

Either find a couple of cotton sheets, one to lie on and one to cover you, or make yourself a loose robe. This should be made from cotton or linen, and must be free of animal fibres, buttons and ties.

Prepare your salt water and dispenser.

Step 2

Select a place. Somewhere in your home there is a place that you can make secure. Additionally, it should, if possible, fulfil the following conditions:

There should be a minimum of clutter. Books, newspapers and other items that give off their own vibrations or elicit specific emotional responses in you should be removed. They are undesirable because of the thought patterns they may engender.

The place should be away from heavy electrical wiring for it has been demonstrated that the currents carried by wiring interfere with the separation of 'I' from 'Me'.

A place near the sky is most desirable. In warm weather, this might be a patio, in winter, an attic room would serve well.

The light level in your area should be adjustable so that during your attempted astral trips it can be lowered to the level you would expect to get from a single lighted candle.

Step 3

Write down the most insistent demand that 'Me' is making on

'I' at the moment. (This step is designed to satisfy 'Me' that it will get its reward for allowing 'I' to leave.)

Write down all the niggling problems you may be having in your mundane life. Place this minor worry-list in the oven and weight it down with your iron. Close the oven door. As you do so, make the following affirmation:

> I lay aside my mundane cares.
> Returning I will attend to them.
> With knowledge gained in a brief respite
> I will be better equipped to lead this life.
> As I will, so mote it be.

Step 4

Step 3 is designed to give you mental homeostasis and to satisfy 'Me' that the physical needs will be taken care of right after the astral flight. The paradox of this is that the insistent demand will be used as the driving force or Defined Necessity that will help you get out of your body. The two most important needs that can be used in this way are sexual fulfilment and hunger.

Taking each in turn:

Sex – If you are sexually frustrated and you have decided to use this as a Defined Necessity in getting 'I' out of the body, then stay frustrated. Otherwise you should make love not more than two hours before your attempt.

Hunger – If you are literally starving, you can use this as a Defined Necessity to get 'I' out of the body. However, we believe that very few people are really that hungry, so we recommend that about one hour before your attempt you have a 'Texas-style' breakfast: a small steak with two fried eggs. We urge you to avoid coffee, and drink instead plain water: to each glass of water add two tablespoons of honey and two tablespoons of vinegar.

The hunger we are talking about here is the type of hunger

you see in an Indian fakir, the hunger that causes him to appear – and to be – near death. If you are honestly in this situation, then you can use hunger as a Defined Necessity; otherwise have the breakfast.

Step 5

For the trial run you do not need to decide what Defined Necessity will finally get you out of your body. However, at this point in the real attempts you must write down what it is you urgently need and take that piece of paper into the circle with you.

Step 6

At last you are ready for the trial run. Let us say you have selected 11 p.m. as the best time for your attempt. Hopefully you have made love at about 9 p.m. and eaten at about 10 p.m. You have all the cares of the day and all the problems neatly written down and placed under the iron in the oven in the kitchen. Shower or bathe; beardless men should also shave. Put on your clean robe if you have one, and go to your selected secure area. Lie with your head to the east on your back on the mattress. If you have one, set your timer for fifteen minutes. Make sure that you can stay quiet for this length of time without being disturbed by any outside noises or influences and, further, that your body doesn't get cramp or pains induced by your posture. If you are disturbed in any way, get up and go and fix whatever the problem may be. Your goal is relaxation and security. Be comfortable – though not so comfortable that you immediately fall asleep. Don't be afraid to make changes in your location, and at this stage do not attempt to astral travel; for you have made no protective affirmations.

It usually takes six or seven trial runs to get everything set.

If you seem to have all sorts of problems during this period, do not be surprised or discouraged. Remember: 'Me' is like a fractious child. It will do all sorts of things to prevent you from keeping your appointment. Our records show fantastic events that can all be traced to 'Me's' fears of 'I's' departure: bank deposits made in error, causing overdrawn accounts; little accidents; you name it, we've seen it. Be persistent. Practise. Eventually, after a couple of weeks at the most, 'Me' will let you go.

Your Flow Chart of Astral Meditation

Figure 4.3 shows a step-by-step breakdown of this seemingly complex but actually simple procedure that we call meditative-state astral travel. The chart also includes a requirement to define your meditative goal (Step 7). Parts 7a, 7b and 7c are described in our Witchcraft course or are available to you by attending a good meditation class. None of these paths, of course, leads to astral travel. Look now at Figure 4.3, starting at the top of the page at Step 1. This step is easily accomplished, of course. When you get to Step 2, however, you see you have two paths: either 'YES' downward, which leads to Step 3, or alternatively, 'NO'. To the right of the 'NO' you will see instructions you should follow so that your development can continue.

Following the steps in their logical sequence leads you naturally into your first astral trip. Be sure that you take these steps every time you trip out.

1. START
   ↓
2. HAVE YOU STUDIED INSTRUCTIONS? → NO → Go back and study
   YES
   ↓
3. IS YOUR MATTRESS COMFORTABLE? → NO → Get a new mattress
   YES
   ↓

4. IS YOUR AREA SECURE? → NO →Arrange a secure area
   YES
   ↓
5. IS YOUR MIND AT EASE? → NO →Prepare worry list
   YES
   ↓
6. HAVE YOU SUCCESSFULLY COMPLETED TRIAL RUN? → NO→ Make necessary adjustments and complete trial run
   YES
   ↓
7. DEFINE MEDITATIVE GOAL:
   a. Inner serenity → Go to eastern-style meditation class
   b. Spiritual serenity → Go to Witchcraft Lecture II
   c. Getting answers to questions → same as b
   d. ASTRAL TRAVEL →   → PROCEED TO STEP 8
   ↓ ←
8. DEFINE NECESSITY
   ↓
9. HAVE YOU SATISFIED 'ME'S' NEEDS, ESPECIALLY SEX AND HUNGER? → NO → Satisfy 'Me's' needs as far as possible. If sex or hunger is Necessity, do not satisfy these needs
   YES
   ↓
10. COMPLETE PROTECTION
    ↓
11. HAVE YOU ESTABLISHED YOUR KEY? → NO → Establish key signal
    YES
    ↓
12. NARROW THOUGHTS TO KEY SIGNAL AND NECESSITY
    ↓
13. ARE YOU RELAXED? →NO→ Return to appropriate step to complete relaxation
    YES
    ↓
14. ASTRAL TRAVEL→NO→ Return to Step 12
    YES
    ↓
15. RETURN FROM ASTRAL TRAVEL
    ↓
16. REMELD 'I' AND 'ME'
    ↓
17. STOP! → Write down experiences →this minute!

Figure 4.3
Flow Chart of Steps to Astral Travel

Your First Keyed Meditative-State Astral Trip

Your preparations are complete. You have reached Step 11 of Figure 4.3. All your cravings, except perhaps the one you are going to use as your urgent Necessity, are moderately satisfied. There is nothing pulling at you, either mentally or physically. There is no possibility of interruption, and you are safe. The light level is comfortably low and no harsh noises penetrate to your ears. Lie on your mattress, resting and waiting. Place your arms at your sides with the palms facing upwards. Now begin to think of what it is you have defined as your Necessity; and at the same time, think about your key signal. Imagine the key signal happening to you; for example, let us say your key is a low buzzing in the centre of your forehead. Concentrate on the centre of your forehead. Imagine it buzzing. Even roll your eyes back and try to look at the centre of your forehead while you think of it buzzing. Relax a moment. Now concentrate all your effort on thinking about your Necessity; then concentrate again on your key signal. Whatever that key signal is, make it happen to your body. Continue this alternation between Necessity and key signal concentration for about five minutes. In this time you should have switched between the two concentrated efforts about ten times; that is, you spent a series of thirty-second increments in each mode of concentration. The last mode of concentration should be on your key signal The more real this can become to you, the more easily you will get out.

Now relax. Let everything slow down from the effort of concentration. Relax every part of your body. Start with your feet and feel them relax so that all the tension flows out. Once they are relaxed, relax your legs. Continue up the body. Unless sex is your urgent Necessity, it is most important in this effort that you thoroughly relax the genitalia. When you have relaxed every body part, think about your breathing. Slow it down, slower and slower. When you've got it as slow and deep as you can comfortably manage, gently return to concentrating on your key signal.

Your experience will now take one of two paths:

PATH 1. Lift out and separate. If your initial type of astral travel is like that of most people, as you are lying on your mattress you will gradually begin to form an astral double that will float above the recumbent 'Me'. In this case, 'I' should gently move away from it. Now with this separation of 'I' and 'Me', begin to think of your Necessity. You should immediately take off, travelling through space in the here-now to the place at which your Necessity can be satisfied. If this does not happen immediately, increase the physical separation between the astral double and 'Me'. Move it out into the street; then begin to concentrate on the Necessity. This requirement for physical separation is well known.

PATH 2. Instant separation. One moment you are lying on your comfortable mattress, and the next instant you are somewhere else. To many people this instant transition is so startling that it jolts them back, but in fact this is one of the better ways to astral travel. You don't have to worry about the separation of a double or a road map to find your way. You will instantly be wherever you want to be. Some people complain that they are not really astral travelling, they are just imagining that they are somewhere else; this is because they do not realize they are actually experiencing instant separation. They believe they are doing what has come to be called 'mental projection'. In the section under 'Record Keeping' we will show you how to tell the difference between real astral travel and mental projection.

You're out! You're flying! Whee! You can go anywhere you like. Nothing can harm you.

Remelding 'I' and 'Me'

Eventually, no matter how much fun you're having, you must return. Do not attempt to think yourself instantly back into your body; instead, come to the door of your secure room, approach 'Me' slowly, and drift down into it. When you get close to your body, you will suddenly snap in. This jolt is somewhat disconcerting for some people, for its intensity varies from subject to subject. Some subjects report hardly any jolt at all. Others report occasions when their return resembles a heavy slap on the back combined with a push in the face. None of these jolts causes any physical damage or problems.

You are now ready to get up and leave your protective circle. Because the circle is a psychic barrier, it contains and keeps the energies that are created from your thoughts. When you break the circle, the retained energies are released. It is usual to direct any energies that may be left over towards some good purpose by saying an affirmation like,

> I ask this great unseen healing force
> To remove all obstructions from my mind and body
> And to restore me to perfect health.
> As I will, so mote it be.

Record Keeping

Even if you think you have no trip to report, even if it seems you have just experienced a hole in time, still, whatever happened, you must make a record. Without that record, you will never know whether or not you are progressing. The record must contain two parts:

1. *Astral experience* – Record specifically what happened while you were lying on your mattress between the time you last remember thinking of your key signal and the

time when you reawoke. Remember, you may not be clairvoyant; so you should record every sensation you have, whether the sensation was in a visual format, or came as a smell, a feeling or a sound.

2. *Mundane results* — Seven days after your astral projection, you should make a record of what has happened in your life in connection with your defined urgent Necessity. Has, for instance, a new friend come into your life, in response to a Necessity of 'Cure loneliness'? Has money come into your life in response to a Necessity of 'Need money'? Whatever has happened in connection with the Necessity, write it down. You may be amazed, looking back over your records, at how your astral projection has affected your mundane life.

In all your record keeping, be sure to date every event. If you wish to do research at a later point in time, or to ask us about your results, we will also expect you to have recorded the times of the events and the phases of the moon when the events occurred. It takes only a few moments to jot down this information but if you don't do it at the time, it can often be very difficult to remember later.

We are most insistent on record keeping because so many people swear to us in all sincerity that their astral trips never happen and that the whole procedure is a fake and not worth the effort. In fact when we examine even their memories of what happened during the projection, and the record of subsequent events in the days following the attempts, we find that significant changes have occurred which could only be the result of a real astral projection.

CHAPTER 5
Anywhere Anytime Astral Travel

Chinese philosopher say: 'Longest journey begin with single step.' You have now taken that single step, and you are entitled to feel proud of the work you have done. Very few people have the perseverence to accomplish controlled astral travel. To review the steps you have taken, look at Figure 5.1. Here are the things you have done.

1. You have remembered your dream-state travel.

2. You have travelled in the twilight-zone.

3. You have travelled in the meditative state.

The next step on your journey is to learn to astral travel when you are not in the safe security of your own space.

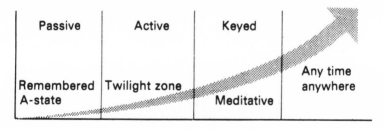

Figure 5.1
Your Growing Ability

Development

Just as an athlete ties weights to his limbs in training, then can run faster when they are removed, so in the development of meditative astral travel you add distractions. When they

are removed you can develop to another level. In the safety
and security of your own circle you should apply distractions
during your astral-travel sessions. The distraction that will
affect you most is dependent on your principal mode of
sensing impressions. The following table of distractions,
Table 5.1, is designed for clairvoyants. If you are clair-
something else, you should change the list so that the first
distraction you apply is not keyed to your principal sensory
input.

Distraction	*How to Increase Distraction Levels*
TOUCH	In your original practice circle you either wore a comfortable robe or were covered by a sheet blanket. In adding touch-distractions, you can first wear tight clothes and then set the room thermostat so that the temperature will rise or fall while you are travelling.
EMOTION	The easiest way to introduce an emotional distraction into your environment is to take something into your circle that reminds you of a violent annoyance. An example of this might be a bounced cheque or some cherished object that has been broken.
SOUND	Start by having your tape recorder play soft music. Change the music to a more insistent rhythm, now change it to a higher volume. As a last test, have the tape recorder switch on a loud raucous noise while you are astrally travelling.
SMELL	The most threatening smell to 'Me' is that of burning. It is a simple matter to arrange a small charcoal barbecue grill and place on it something that will first smoulder and then ignite while 'I' is in the astral.
LIGHT	Increase the light level in your circle until it is as

bright as day. Then set up a Christmas-tree flasher
to flash lights at you as you astral travel.

Table 5.1
Controlled Distractions

You will notice that 'taste' is not mentioned in the table.
Unless the circumstances are extremely unusual, there will be
no taste distraction when you are meditatively astral travelling. For instance, it is most unlikely that when you are sitting
in a crowded tube station someone will come over and
introduce a flavour into your mouth. If someone did attempt
such a feat, 'Me' would obviously perceive such an act as an
imminent threat and would bring 'I' back instantly.

The key to learning to astral travel with various distractions present is the realization of the fact that what you are
really doing is convincing 'Me' that none of the distractions
constitute a threat to 'Me's' well-being. 'Me' must learn to
recognize, identify and accept the distractions for what it is,
then let it go. For instance, when 'Me' hears loud, raucous
noises from the tape recorder, it must accept them. It must
say to itself, 'That's the tape recorder. It presents no threat. I
can go about my business without caring.' It is surprising
how few people can accept no-threat sounds in their daily life.
The barking dog, the yelling neighbour, the plane overhead, all
are sources of annoyance. If you can learn instead to identify the
noise, accept it and let it go without caring, your life will be far
more comfortable.

It is important to your success in this effort to recognize
that the technique described here is not one of establishing
blocks. When you block something out, you cut off part of
your receptivity and awareness. Doing this may block out
some of those faint sensory signals that indicate you are
astral travelling. Do not clench up and resist sensory inputs;
instead, identify and accept, all the time reassuring 'Me' that

these inputs are non-threatening. You may think of this as a game that 'I' plays with 'Me'. 'I' is saying, 'Stay on duty, "Me". Be aware. Soon I will be back, and I expect my body still to be in good shape.'

Psychic Protection

So that you can astrally trip out anywhere you find yourself, you must develop a simple and effective means of putting up psychic bars that will convince 'Me' it is safe to let 'I' go. The bars must be strong enough to convince discarnate entities as well that this body is not available for possession. Reflective talismans[1] have been used since time immemorial to serve this purpose. Experiments at the Canterbury Institute show that in most cases 'Me' feels secure when the head, the solar plexus, the hands and the feet are psychically protected, though some subjects felt the additional need of protection in the neck or heart area. When you arrange these protection devices, you are creating a disturbance in the natural fields around you. This disturbance works in the same way as any of the sensory irregularities listed in Table 5.2. Thus when you first make and use your talismans, you will have to learn how to astral travel with them on just as you learned to astral travel in the presence of other sensory distractions. There will be a temporary lowering of your ability when you first wear a full set of your protective talismans, but this is natural and will quickly be overcome.

Protecting the Brain and the Head

That most sensitive computer, the brain, can easily be directly influenced by psychic energies. It appears that the majority of these energies flow in through what is called the

[1] As the Canterbury Institute uses the word 'talisman', it means 'any scientifically designed shielding device'.

'third eye', the place in centre-forehead that high-caste Hindus protect with the red caste mark. The leather skullcap of an orthodox Jew makes an excellent protector for the rest of the head. Many centuries ago it was found that an iron band wrapped in leather forms a total protective circle when it is placed on the head. When under direct psychic attack, many trained occultists rely on protection of this type. In astral travel it is better not to use leather because, coming as it does from an animal that died in pain and terror, leather has its own emotional energies that may hinder your perception of astral-travel messages. Using four turns of galvanized wire wrapped in a cotton band, as shown in Figure 5.2, has proved totally effective.

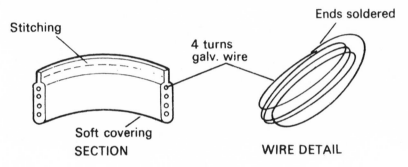

Figure 5.2
Your Protective Headband
(normally worn under a hat)

Protecting the Heart

The most simple protective device you can use is a necklace made of iron or silver wire. A more powerful heart protector is a flat circular disc of iron hung as a medallion from the necklace, arranged so that it lies over the heart. Most subjects like to have this talisman engraved. A suitable engraving is shown in Figure 5.3; this particular design is said to have originated with King Solomon.

Protecting the Hands

There are two ways to do this. First, you might choose to
wear on each wrist a bracelet of solid iron. The Sikhs favour
this method of protection and have such bracelets welded on
before they go into battle. Alternatively, finger rings can be
used. A single ring on the ring finger of each hand has been
found to be adequate. Plain silver or iron rings with simple
designs engraved like that shown in Figure 5.4 are preferred.

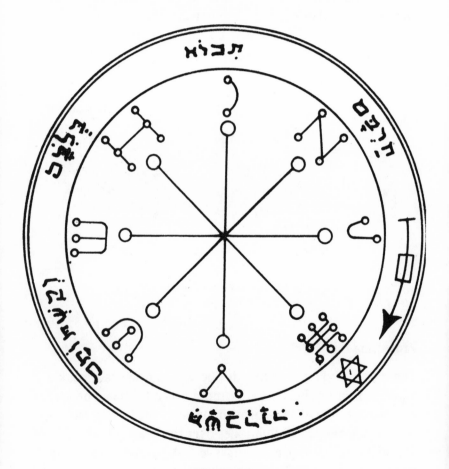

Figure 5.3
Protective Talisman Engraving

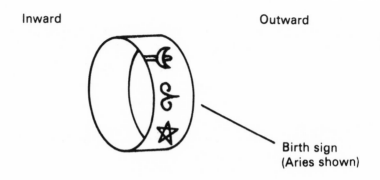

Figure 5.4
Typical Ring Engraving

Protecting the Solar Plexus

A large, ornate belt buckle made of iron is the simplest way of ensuring protection for the original pathway of life force into your body. It should be highly polished; it too can be engraved with the King Solomon design shown in Figure 5.3.

Protecting Your Feet

In everyday life people seem to overlook the need to protect their feet. It is not by chance that leather is used to stop the flow of energy between the ground and the feet. The replacement of leather with synthetic materials has led to an epidemic of tired-foot syndrome. Try it some time. Go out and get yourself a pair of shoes soled in natural leather. You will immediately find that your feet feel better when you wear the natural leather. The best protection for the feet is a pair of moccasins. If these are too distracting, get a pair of iron anklets. Make sure they fit closely around the narrowest part of the ankle but do not impede the natural blood flow.

Learning to Astral Travel in a Fully Protected State

Learn to use your protective talismans in the security of your own circle. Once you can consistently astral travel when you are wearing them all, you can try astral travelling without the protection of your salt circle. It is usual in these cases to imagine yourself surrounded by a circle or cylinder of white light. Wearing your talismans, lie on your mattress and say,

> I am surrounded by the pure white light of the God.
> Nothing but good shall come to me.
> Nothing but good shall go from me.
> I give thanks.
> As I will, so mote it be.

As you say the affirmation, imagine yourself to be surrounded and completely encased in a cylinder of pure blue-white light. If your senses tell you that the cylinder is not complete, try it again. Do not astral travel until you are sure that the blue-white light completely protects you.

Successful Astral Travel under Any Conditions

You have learned how to handle violent distractions to each of your senses in turn. You have learned how to astral travel while loaded down with protective talismans. Now you can leave the safety of the circle area and start astral travelling first from other rooms in your own home and then from such places as a waiting room. It is just a matter of practice. Do not try, however, to astral travel from a place where 'Me' cannot gauge possible threats or interruptions. This means that astral travelling in an aircraft in flight or on a bus on the road is extremely difficult. Skilled astral travellers can indeed quiet 'Me's' fears sufficiently for 'I' to depart under these circumstances, but you should wait several years before attempting it.

Did You Really Make It Come True?

Was it all a dream? Did it really happen? If you doubt the validity of your experience, return to Page 32 and read the paragraph headed 'Category 3'. This will give you some clues as to whether you were dreaming or really astrally travelling. Another clue that some subjects use is to look for their aka thread. If your travel is of the type where an astral double first separates, you should be able to see the thread connecting the astral double to the mundane body. When you first get out of your body and are close (within 10 metres, (30 feet)), look over your shoulder. Most subjects can clearly see a thread connecting the double to 'Me'. This is a thread of light which usually connects the solar plexus of 'Me' to the back of the head of the double. Seeing this thread is an indisputable verification of the fact that you are really astrally travelling. Remember some subjects detect the thread through senses other than sight.

If you astral travel by the instant-separation method, you will never see an aka thread. In this case, proceed to 'What You Did There' (Page 97). If, on the other hand, you are convinced that you did not astrally travel, then you need to go back to the 'Flow Chart of Steps to Astral Travel' in Figure 4.3. Carefully consider each step, and during your consideration re-read the relevant text paragraphs. Make sure you have not overlooked some simple yet vital instruction. If you have overlooked such an instruction, correct your procedure and try again. Don't become discouraged. It sometimes takes several attempts to make your first trip. This is a whole new, very worthwhile, aspect of life that you are exploring, an aspect that is on the borderline of knowledge. The bicycle-riding simile is still apt: we can give you rules and hints and suggestions, but we really can't tell you in cold text exactly how to ride your bicycle. It's a learned skill. Once you have learned it, it's yours for ever.

Common Causes of Failure

The following are the most usual reasons that subjects fail to get out on their first attempt.

1. *Fear* – No matter how many times we tell people that they have nothing to fear, they still persist in having unnameable, undefined fears. All we can do is tell you that none of our students has ever had the least problem in getting out when they followed our instructions. The only thing we can suggest you do is write down your fear. See whether it is real. In most cases when it is written down it becomes if not ridiculous, at least manageable. Then you can convince your particular 'Me' that its fears are groundless.

2. *Health* – If your 'Me' is in poor health, you should begin taking steps to remedy this problem. Go and see a doctor. We can't do it for you. It is true that just like lack of food or sex, poor health can be used as a Necessity to get you out; but these cases are successful only when the poor health has been evaluated as incurable, irreparable or terminal by orthodox medicine. In cases where you have a fever or a heavy head-cold or something of that nature, wait until it is cured before attempting astral travel.

3. *Electrical Fields* – We cannot say enough about avoiding these hindrances. If you suspect that this is one of your problems, turn the power off in the house. Make sure, too, that you don't have anything around that may be disturbing the natural electro-magnetic field. This includes such things as closed finger-rings, jewellery, hairpins, steel-bladed knives, magnets and a host of other items that disturb the natural fields. It is not by chance that eastern temples are built with no iron in them; nor that in the old days all iron and steel in a village was locked up prior to any religious festival. Make sure before your next attempt

that all such disturbing objects are removed from your environment.

4. *Timing* – The aim of keyed meditative-state astral travel is to allow you to trip out on key at any time. But again, it's like riding a bicycle. You wouldn't try to learn to ride a bicycle in the middle of the high street or at the top of a steep hill; though once you have learned to ride, of course you can ride up and down hills and along the high street. The same rule holds true in astral travel. It is easier to travel when the sun is below the horizon. It is also easier to travel when the moon is full. Try to arrange it, therefore, so that your first attempt occurs at around midnight near full moon.

5. *Clock, Calendar and Telephone* – The things that keep you in your mundane body are clock, calendar and telephone, and the worries they engender. 'Me' must learn that 'I' has to have time to itself just as 'Me' needs time to eat, drink and be merry. If all else fails, take a holiday. Get away from it all. Go somewhere quiet that has no telephone. Leave your clock and calendar at home. If your family fights you on this, leave them at home too.

What You Did There

Your travelling should have been in the here-now. In this realm the physical landscape in unchanged. From your point of view, the only difference is that you can easily pass through physical objects and you can see the spirit or ghost population of the physical world. Other 'I's' tripping out are part of this population. These other spirits are solid, real objects that you can bump into.

In your travels about the world in your new state, you can do many things you have always wanted to: spy on the neighbours, go and see what the Queen and Prince Philip are doing, watch your MP. This is fun, and we encourage you to do it; but once you have got over this initial phase of exuberant investigation, you should settle down to more serious work.

In Chapter 4 we spoke of fulfilling both sexual and nutritional needs. Now it is time for you to find the answers to the questions that will help you fulfil your Necessity.

Often subjects report that they went to a place which seemed to have no connection with a solution to their problems. If you defined your Necessity correctly, the place you go to always had a connection with the Necessity. No matter how unrelated it may seem to be, there will be a reason why you are visiting this particular spot during your astral trip. You must remember in detail everything you can about the place you visit. Below is a list of things that subjects have found useful in keying their memories and in identifying a solution to their problems.

1. *Type of housing* – This gives a clue as to the location of the trip.

2. *Types of cars* – Again, a location clue. Do everything you can to remember the registration numbers and the types and makes of vehicles you see.

3. *Newspapers* – If they are in a language you understand, read the headlines. Notice particularly the date of publication; for you may have unwittingly moved out of the here-now. Obviously if you are trying to overcome a problem of loneliness, you will pay special attention to photographs and names of likely companions which appear in the paper. Sometimes our astrals play tricks, and you may find yourself confronted with a whole stack of newspapers. In this case, think, 'Stop that nonsense! Tell me what I want to know!' In nine cases out of ten, you will then be redirected.

4. *People* – Whom did you see? Usually the first person you see is the one who holds the key to solving your problem. You should do everything you can to identify this person. Look for names on letters or documents; even nametags in clothing and on luggage have been known to serve as a link so that you can find the person after you have returned to the mundane world.

5. *Business offices and factories* – This usually means that you are supposed to seek employment at these locations. They are the easiest of all to find when you are back in the mundane because they will have signs on the doors or at the gate.

We cannot tell you in advance all the myriad places that you may visit on your astral travels, nor can we tell you the meaning of the places you visit. You have to keep your head in gear and decide for yourself what the true meaning of all these experiences will prove to be.

Long-Term Results

Some subjects find that they get no immediate results. This is because the veil between the astral and the mundane is more firmly closed in their case than it is with 90 percent of people. Even though you have no recollection in any of your senses that you have astral travelled, you have tripped out. One sure way of verifying this is to note the changes in your life that occur in the week following your attempt. Notice particularly any changes associated with your Necessity – in many cases you will find that it has been magically fulfilled.

Over the years we have found another conspicuous and valuable result of these astral trips is the serenity and peace that come into the lives of the subjects as a result of their attempts. This serenity is quite startling in its contrast to the former hectic disturbed lifestyle of the subject. We get letters almost every day saying essentially, 'Even though my Necessity was fulfilled, and for that I am grateful, I am far more grateful for the serenity that my work and your course have given me.'

Follow-up

In astral travel as in many other things in life, you must follow the leads that you are given. You will find that if you do not follow them, you lose the ability to astral travel on key and to get answers to Necessities. We don't really know why this is. Recently, several occultists have theorized that it stops working because 'Me' simply refuses to risk 'I' leaving when 'I' doesn't bother or is too spineless to follow up on the results obtained in this very special way. For now, we are using this hypothesis as a law. We can definitely say that if you do not follow up on the leads 'I' gets, then 'Me' will interfere with the smooth transition into the astral that is the whole aim of this work you are doing.

Summary

To date you have learned two methods of astral travel. In order to clarify their use and differences, we are summarizing them for you here. Future chapters are based on the assumption that you will be able to travel in the astral on a regular basis; so this is the point where you need to stop and take stock.

1. TWILIGHT ZONE – A-State
    Easiest and most natural mode of astral travel.
    Cannot be done on demand, for it requires the presence of a protecting Guide who will look after 'Me' while 'I' is out. 'Me' goes to sleep while 'I' stays awake. (Many

meditative schools use this fact to help get 'I' out. They require that their students do heavy physical labour without any mental effort; thus 'Me' goes to sleep quite readily while 'I' is still active.)

2. MEDITATIVE STATE

More difficult than Twilight Zone.

Can be done on command, in response to key signals.

Protection is done in the physical plane; consequently no Guide is required.

'I' and 'Me' are both awake. 'Me' is homeostatic; that is, most or all of 'Me's' demands are satisfied.

An urgent Necessity is required to get 'I' out.

Remember that whatever results you get must be recorded. In this way your own record will show you that your Necessities are being met and that permanent changes are coming into your life on a long-term basis.

CHAPTER 6
The Here-Now and the Space-Time Continuum

The astral is a vast realm that you could explore for ever. This book makes no pretence of covering every possible combination of places you can visit, but purely for convenience we have divided the astral into five easily understood locations which we call realms.

The five astral realms we have defined are:

HERE-NOW — This is the realm to which you usually go in your A-state dreaming. It is congruent with the presently existent physical world. In foregoing chapters you have been learning to travel about it, seeing friends at their daily tasks and visiting any part of it you wish.

TIME — You have occasionally visited this realm in your travels. You travel forwards and backwards in time, still in the here-now. Some rather startling changes in your view of the real world occur when you astral travel in time. The changes that we have found to date are outlined for you in this chapter.

COSMIC — These are the far realms of the physical world. Using this form of astral travel, you can find out for yourself whether or not other planets in other solar systems are inhabited and, if so, what the life forms look like.

HERE-NOW GUIDANCE — These are the teaching realms in the spirit world. They are very useful realms, for from them you can get answers to many of your questions. We suspect they are the realms from which both ancient and modern civilizations gained much of their knowledge. When an inventor is stuck, he can go here to get guidance. When a writer's manuscript goes 'cold', he too can get the information he needs to continue working.

SPIRITUAL — This realm has many planes of ever-increasing spirituality. It is a joyful, beautiful place, one where you will dwell when you 'die'. Exploration of these planes removes all fear of death from your mundane consciousness. The upper Nirvana-like realms are available and waiting for you to visit today. A fuller description of these realms is in Chapter 7.

Astral Gateways

One of the methods that has been used since earliest time to understand the differences between the various realms is the gateway concept.

The gateways we shall use in this book are:

Gate 1 This is the gate through which you pass to the astral here-now. It is the one through which you go naturally in your A-state dreaming.

Gate 2 Occasionally you have already passed into different time zones in your astral travels. Gateway 2 leads to travel forwards and backwards in time in realms that are congruent to the earth plane.

Gate 3 This is the gateway to the cosmos. You are still travelling in realms that are congruent to the physically existing cosmos.

Gate 4 This is the first gateway through which you progress towards higher spiritual realms. It is the gate from the here-now to the cultural realms.

Gate 5 This gate is sometimes called 'beauty itself'. It leads from the cultural realms upwards into the variable realms and the judgment area.

The last human gateway is so indefinable that it is not given a mundane number. It leads a human melded entity out of the completed human experience.

The Here-Now

Any time you leave your body and travel in the astral here-now, you will see a large population of other spiritual beings travelling in the same realm. The beings are of four types:

1. Spirits like yourself who will return to their bodies. This general class of spirits might be called 'souls' or incarnated spirits.
2. Spirits of dead people. These are loosely referred to as 'ghosts' or spirits. They are discarnate because they have no bodies to return to. Many of them appear lost or concerned. They often rush around aimlessly. A small percentage of them are more distraught and confused than the others; these are spirits of the most recently dead, to whom the death experience has been unusually traumatic and confusing.
3. Thoughtforms. These make up the most startling and unexpected things you come across in the realm. Sometimes they take on fantastic shapes. They are the product of people's minds: crystallized thoughtforms. Mostly they are visualizations of gods and goddesses, but some are just clouds of angry energy. The oldest of them appear faint, but others are quite dense; they should all be avoided.
4. Little People. These are the group spirits of natural forces. They can take on multitudinous forms, but generally you can classify them into four groups.

a) Salamanders. These are fire spirits; there is usually one in every home. Most of them are friendly. You will find large fire spirits near volcanoes and other natural fiery phenomena. Pele is a typical powerful salamander from Hawaii.

b) Gnomes. This category includes not just gnomes but also other 'little people' such as pixies, elves and leprechauns. They are of the earth. You will find them where the earth has been torn apart by modern construction work, or in caves, and near such earth anomalies as the San Andreas Fault in California.

c) Sylphs. These are spirits of the air, and are to be found most frequently at the times when equinoctial storms occur; that is, during the hurricane season in the Caribbean and during the tornado season in the American midwest. They are found in other parts of the world during their respective storm seasons, and anywhere hot and cold air currents meet.

d) Undines. These water spirits are storm-generated beings associated with tumbling, rather than placid, waters. They are to be found in abundance at a waterfall, at a whirlpool, at storm centres, or in the Portland Race on the English Channel.

Certain things are not found in this realm. Most noticeable among these are the spirits of animals, plants or any life form other than that of humankind. You may occasionally see someone who appears to have the spirit of an animal accompanying him; but this is not an animal spirit. Instead it is a thoughtform the human spirit has created for himself so he can enjoy the same kind of companionship he shared with an animal on the earth plane. The absence of non-human spirits has led philosophers to place man on a higher level than other creatures. For centuries it has been assumed that man is above – and therefore rules and controls – all other life forms. Philosophers now believe that there are parallel here-nows for every other form of creature. Until now explorations of these other here-now realms have been only random occurrences enjoyed in no predictable way by a few subjects. The steps for getting into such realms are not in any way established or known. Judging by reports we have received from the few subjects who have made it, there is no danger or problem in those realms.

Simplistic Representation of the Astral Here-Now

Grasping the reality of the astral here-now is sometimes difficult for those of us who would like an exact, guaranteed picture of the way it is. Unfortunately such a picture is not possible, because subjects construct their own interpretation of what they experience during astral trips. Figure 6.1 is one simplistic way of explaining the astral here-now. The figure shows it as an area of finite depth seemingly hovering over another area of finite depth that is the 'real', physical world[1]. These two are actually congruent, the one fitting perfectly into the other. We have separated the two planes and made them of finite dimensions merely for the sake of the illustration. In fact, they spread out into the infinity of space in all directions. The gate that we have called Gateway 1 is your entrance from the existent physical world into the astral here-now. As soon as you enter the astral here-now, you are at, let us say, Point A in the figure. Now you can elect to astral travel about the existent physical world; you can elect to travel in time into the future or the past; or you can elect to travel upwards into the spiritual realms. For convenience only, the spirit realms are shown upward, the existent

---

[1]'Real', 'physical', 'existent', and 'mundane' are synonymous terms for the plane where 'Me' dwells, the plane where you earn your living.

physical world is shown horizontally, and the future/past
dimension is shown perpendicular to the other two. Although
the axes are arbitrary, it is convenient to think of the spirit
realms as upward and travelling in the existent world
(whether it be in your own time zone or in the past or future)
as horizontal; for it is in this horizontal world that emotional
links to the mundane still exist and spirits consequently tend
to retain many behaviour patterns of a non-spiritual nature.

Geographically, the astral here-now is identical to the
physical world. Thus when you travel in time, the geography
still remains the same (apart from minor changes of a man-
made or geological nature). This geographical sameness also
carries over into cosmic astral travel.

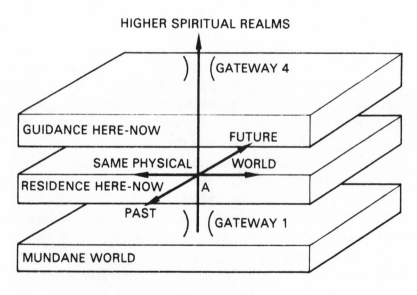

Figure 6.1
Pictorial Representation of the Astral Here-Now

The figure shows three levels. The lowest level shown is the
mundane world; above that is an astral residence level, which
we have been calling the 'astral here-now'; and above that
again is a level we call 'guidance'. There is no barrier or

gateway between the residence and the guidance levels, yet the guidance level is definitely different from the residence level. The representations of the real world in a geographical sense start to fade. Artificially created, vaguely outlined settings that resemble lecture halls are superimposed on the here-now, and are more real than many of the mundane-world outlines. There is also an abundance of small garden settings and bench-type arrangements. These settings are designed for guidance.

When you have questions to be answered, and have used them as a defined urgent necessity, you will automatically find yourself in one of these small teaching arrangements. If you are patient, this is where you will receive the answers you seek. Patience is most important, for with it even the most complex ideas can be clarified.

The guides or astral sages who visit the guidance level appear much larger than life. They are in fact progressed, melded spirits who come down from higher levels to help guide the less developed. By doing this guidance counselling, they themselves in turn learn and progress further. The guidance is not done in any verbal or overt, outward way. To a viewer not part of the communication group, nothing visible is going on. When you step into a group you become aware of the telepathic flow of ideas and information transfer that is happening.

Notice that in Figure 6.1 no downward direction is indicated. In analysis of reports from hundreds of subjects we have found only two that discussed a downward-into-hell experience. We believe that these two subjects created this hell-like reality for themselves, probably because they had been so strongly imprinted with the idea of hell from funda-mentalist Christian parents. If you find a hell-like domain, we would very much like to know how you did it and its attributes as you perceive them.

Two useful, if somewhat confusing, facts about the astral

here-now may help you to pin down your location when you are astral travelling.

1. Light-levels – Astral day and night are brighter than day and night in the mundane world. During astral day light is quite intense, and during astral night it is still possible to see clearly.

2. Sleep time – You will occasionally notice newly arrived spirits who seem to be dormant or sleeping. This is because they do not realize that sleep in unnecessary in the astral here-now.

Discarnate Spirits in the Astral Here-Now

There seems to be tremendous random activity among the discarnate spirits in the astral here-now. When you can telepathically communicate with one of these discarnates, you will usually find that the dominant emotion is puzzlement. They wonder where they are and what they are doing. Tens of millions of spirits inhabit the lowest here-now level, and seem never to progress or be interested in progressing.

Why people from the residence areas do not readily avail themselves of the guidance level, is a mystery to most students of astral travel. Obstinacy, fear, indifference to development – whatever it is, it seems a pity. The old Hermetic teaching, 'When the student is ready, the teacher will appear,' is totally applicable in the residence plane of the astral here-now. As soon as anyone in that residence plane feels a desire for guidance, he moves into a guidance centre where a Sage will help him. A careful astral observer will sometimes notice the abrupt disappearance of a discarnate spirit in the middle of a telepathic question-and-answer period. What has happened? The discarnate has suddenly realized where it is and what it is doing; and with this 'aha!' realization it is able to progress to a higher spiritual realm. Many reasons keep discarnates in the residence level:

1. The residence level of the astral here-now is not a teaching or guiding realm. Instead it is a transitory place, a way-station on the way to higher realms. For reasons we do not yet understand, guidance from higher does not come down into this realm. Instead the spirits must move on when a self-realization 'aha' experience comes to them.

2. Many spirits feel safe in this realm. It is much like the earth plane they have left. They can watch loved ones, they can go to church, they can do many of the things they're used to. This is why you may observe clusters of them at church sites.

3. Some spirits are still emotionally bonded to living people or to places. They want to see how Little Janie grows up. They want to watch over that husband to make sure he isn't unfaithful to them. There are a million little emotional bonds that can tie spirits into the residence level. You can help them progress by telepathically talking to them about their emotional bonds.

4. Spirits having unfinished business on the earth plane try desperately to finish that business. Typical cases are far too numerous to go into, but one that we experienced will illustrate our meaning. It involved a little girl who had been told she would never go to heaven unless she could read. Because she could not read, she 'knew' she could not progress.

5. Spirits do not change their character when they pass through Gateway 1. Often you will find spirits behaving with unbelievable obstinacy. Since 'heaven' is not the way they thought it would be, they refuse to take note of their surroundings or to believe there will be other realms of existence to which they can progress. We find the most demure little old ladies with this trait: 'It's not like the vicar told me it was going to be. I'm waiting for him so I

can give him a piece of my mind. And wait they do, even though the vicar has long since passed through this realm and beyond it.

6. The discovery of sex and sexuality in 'heaven' is a great surprise to many spirits – not to mention a delight! Once they understand this aspect of the here-now residence environment, they can't get enough of sexual melding. Years of frustration result in an over-reaction to a situation where both sexes literally wear their desires on their sleeve. There is no such thing as guilt, infidelity or false modesty. Contrary to earth plane stereotypes, if a female spirit wishes to meld, it is quite obvious from one glance at her aura. In some cases this melding activity continues for many years. While spirits are enjoying themselves and making up for lost time, they are not interested in higher development.

Many altruistic incarnate spirits spend years helping discarnates overcome their reluctance to leave the familiarity of the astral here-now. Sometimes this takes discussions with loved ones on the earth plane who are still clinging to the discarnate; a widow who is helpless without her husband – although he died ten years ago – is a typical example of this clinging, cloying 'love' bond that prevents the husband's spirit from progressing.

Cosmic Astral Projection

Projecting into the cosmos is one of the easiest extensions of your here-now ability. You are still travelling in the here-now, even though you are travelling many millions of light-years. Nothing in space can harm you; even projecting on to the surface of the sun or into its centre has no effect on your astral entity. All you have to do to travel to another planet is to establish in your mind what place you wish to visit. Again, the more accurate your perception of the destination, the more accurate and quick will be your arrival there. Recent space photographs of other planets have been a great help to most subjects in projecting themselves to the planets. You should not travel to some imaginary location. If you imagine a sci-fi-type world and then try to travel to it, you will actually travel inside your own mind, for the place you have imagined exists only within your mind. This can be frustrating, until you realize what is happening. Remember when you are travelling in the here-now that you must go to real places; otherwise you will stay for ever inside your own head.

Astral Projection in the Time Domain

Travelling in time is a very easy accomplishment. You must now decide on a destination and a generalized time frame that you would like to visit. In aiming at a time long ago or in the far future, some subjects find that visualizing a calendar with the pages being torn off and blown away in the wind helps them to arrive at their target time. For shorter time-travel journeys, it is useful to imagine a clock face with the hands rapidly turning forwards or backwards. In the next paragraph we are going to discuss 'zonal time'. For now, just remember that it is not always possible to get to the precise date and time that you aim at. This seems to be a universal law of our reality. We have no explanation for it. To summarize time travel, all you have to do is think of the general date and the place, and establish your own Necessity for being there. Then you will arrive quicky and easily at your destination.

Zonal Time

When you attempt to travel either forwards or backwards in time, you will find that you can go only to certain, apparently cyclical, time locations. We have insufficient data to establish whether or not these time windows are fixed for all observers or whether they vary from subject to subject. This means, for instance, from one subject's observations, that you cannot travel to a place that is two hours ahead of you; but you can travel to a place that is approximately a week ahead of you. Similarly, one subject could not travel two or three weeks ahead, but could travel a month ahead.

Statistical evidence shows that the further you go into the future, the longer the cycles get; so that, whereas you may be able to travel one year ahead, you will not be able to get into the time zone that is two to three years ahead but can visit ten or even five hundred years ahead. Similar 'windows in time' exist as you travel into the past.

Figure 6.2 is a graphic representation of this cyclical time phenomenon. The lower line represents time running forwards and backwards. The zigzag zones are the zones into which you can travel – your time windows. The straight zones are zones that you cannot reach today. Please understand that their location and length are as yet not defined. Whereas the general pattern is statistically correct for all observers, the detail has not been sufficiently analysed to say whether or not it is the same for all. This whole pattern shifts every day as 'future' crosses 'present' and becomes 'past'. Tomorrow you will be able to travel into new time zones but will lose access to old ones. The new time zones you can now visit may overlap a little of the old time zones; but soon the time zone into which you were able to travel last week is gone from you until the cycle brings it back into coincidence. Many explanations have been suggested for this phenomenon; the most common is that our reality intersects the realities of other time zones at continuously changing locations. As you will find in the questions in this book, we are leaving it up to you to explore this phenomenon and establish your own explanation.

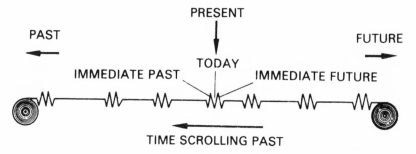

PRESENT

PAST FUTURE

TODAY

IMMEDIATE PAST IMMEDIATE FUTURE

TIME SCROLLING PAST

⎰⎱ represent areas you can visit during astral travel. (Only seven are shown in illustration; there are many more available.)

――― represents areas you cannot visit. Note: The further you move away from the present, the longer these areas become.

Figure 6.2
Graphic Illustration of Zonal Time

Some other puzzling phenomena occur in time travelling, and we have been at a loss to know why they have not been reported in the occult literature. Far be it from us to say that most books on astral projection are fakes; however, we do have serious doubts about the authenticity of supposed astral projection reports that fail to mention obvious and easily observable time-zone phenomena.

Time in Time

As you progress forwards in time, so time expands or stretches. Let us say you have astrally travelled forward to the year 2500. You will find that you can spend days or even weeks in this time zone and upon your return to your body you will find that only a few minutes have passed in real-world time. When you travel back into history, the opposite effect occurs. That is, if you go back to the 1500s and spend just a few seconds there, when you return to your body you find that several minutes have passed. For the reasons noted below under 'Colour' and 'Sound', most subjects do not like to travel more than a thousand years either forwards or backwards. Obviously it would be most interesting to find a group of subjects willing to travel far into the future, spending many years there in a fifteen-minute real-world span. Taken to its limit, you could spend a whole lifetime in the future while your 'Me' lay waiting.

Colour in Time

When you travel into the here-now, you will notice that your colour perception is slightly dulled; that is, things are not as bright as they look when your 'I' and 'Me' are together in the real world. This phenomenon seems to be responsible for the fact that it is more difficult to see auras in the physical than it is in the astral here-now.

As soon as you travel forward in time, colours become more brilliant — violently so, often psychedelically so. Eventually this intensity of colour, its very density and brilliance, becomes overwhelming and painful to the 'I'. When you travel into history, colours become even more faded than they seem when you view the here-now. The further you go back, the more faded the colours become, until soon the scene appears as on black-on-white monochrome. Even this finally begins to fade, the blacks become fuzzy, the outlines blur. Finally, all is mist. The timing of the place at which you see mist seems to be dependent on the age of the astral traveller. In order to obtain more information on this topic, we are asking you to report on it in the questionnaire at the end of the book.

Sound, Smell and Emotion in Time

Just as in the case of colour, so other sensory inputs change in intensity as you move in time. All become more intense as you move forward and less intense as you move back into history. The increase in emotional energy levels is particularly distressing to many of our more sensitive researchers.

Your Power in Time

You now are familiar with the fact that when you travel in the here-now you have the ability to affect your surroundings; that ability is limited by what we call your astral power. In most subjects this is approximately 56 grams (2 oz). The instant you start to travel back in time you will find that your astral power decreases to zero. You can have no effect whatsoever on the past, for it is immutable.

A moment's thought shows you the logic of this reality. If you could affect the past, you could make dramatic changes in the here-now. For example, if you could interrupt your own conception, you would not be there to interrupt your own conception; for you would not exist in the here-now. Such circular reasoning demonstrates that this concept of time is valid.

When you travel ahead in time, your power dramatically increases. When you have travelled far enough ahead, your astral power begins to approach your mundane real-world power. You can then have as much effect on future scenes as you can have in your own body in the real world.

Divining Your Own Future

Provided you work within the restrictions of zonal-time travel, you can travel ahead into your own future and see what is going to happen in your life. This means that you can get peeps at your own life in the future, getting an occasional glimpse of yourself as you will appear. This snapshot is merely a brief glimpse, comparable to a single paragraph, in the book of your life. Your real future life may be vastly different, either better or worse, than the life you viewed in the snapshot. Do not be too discouraged by the circumstances you see surrounding yourself in the future. Remember, they are still subject to the possibility of change. They are not yet fixed. Things you do today in the real world will affect your future.

Safe Time Travel

These areas have been well explored, and to date no one has ever reported problems in exploring them. We suggest you start with short trips, both forwards and back, then go where you like, exploring the far limits of your capabilities in both directions. It's a whole new world for you to travel safely in. The phenomena we mentioned will aid you in your time travel, for they readily allow you to know where you are.

The same rules apply in time travel that apply in here-now travel. If 'Me' is threatened, you will snap back into the here-now. You need have no fear of getting lost, for you can readily imagine yourself back in your body and instantly you will be pulled towards it.

Summary

The realms are there for you to explore. This exploration can be of great interest to you, and at times can be a source of great entertainment. It is a most serious study, one that is at the very frontier of our knowledge, one that may result in far greater understanding of the intersections of our reality with other similar realities and infinitely expand our universe.

CHAPTER 7
The Spiritual Realms

The answers to philosophical questions like:

WHY ARE WE HERE?

lie not in the astral here-now but in other higher levels.[1] The
first clue you have to these other levels of existence comes
when you observe entities disappear from the here-now
guidance realm.

Discarnate Progress from the Guidance Level

Subjects returning from the guidance level report that
discarnate spirits disappear from that level in two ways:

1. When a single discarnate spirit leaves the level, it returns
   to earth to inhabit a new body. Apparently its learning
   process is not complete, and it must return to the mundane
   earth plane to resume its education.

2. Occasionally subjects have observed the sudden
   disappearance of three discarnate spirits at one time; the
   spirits meld together, form a permanent new entity, and
   then disappear. Discussion with Guides indicates that
   these new beings proceed immediately to a higher plane
   that we at the Institute call the 'residence level of the
   cultural realms'. The cultural realms are similar to the here-
   now and the here-now guidance levels, with the major
   exception that they are not related in any way to the real
   world. Instead they seem to be formed by the group con-

[1]"Higher levels' is conventional terminology used as a matter of convenience. It is not meant to imply 'above'.

sciousness, what is called the 'consensus reality', of the people resident there to suit their own taste.

Melding

Careful observation of the melding phenomenon has shown that the new being consists of two spirits of one gender and one of the other gender; that is, two male spirits meld with one female spirit to make a third spirit, or two female spirits meld with a male spirit to form a third spirit. In general the spirits that meld have a common cultural background.

Melding is shown diagramatically in the lower levels of Figure 7.1. After what we call 'death', the human-level spirit comes to live in the lowest level of the here-now and then receives guidance and counselling in the guidance level of the here-now. It either progresses upwards into higher levels of the spiritual world or returns to the earth plane in a new identity. In order to progress upwards, it must give up part of its egotistical identity; that is, it must become so selfless that it is willing to meld its identity into that of two other beings. In doing so, it also gives up part of its sexuality, but it does not give up its cultural identity.

Figure 7.1 also shows meldings at levels above the here-now. To progress from the cultural realms, entities must learn to release cultural differences and meld with beings from other cultures. In just the same manner that spirits must return to earth to learn, so entities descend from the cultural realms to the here-now to learn through helping spirits who are less developed. We call these higher beings who are not developed enough to progress from the cultural realms Guides. It should be remembered that Guides are also on a ladder of progression and that when they have learned enough they too will proceed to higher levels. Thus Guides disappear just as often as do discarnate spirits resident in the guidance levels.

Myths and folk tales of many cultures hint at the meldings that take place in the spiritual realms. The triple-headed god of Roman and Greek mythology is but one very clear indication that they had good knowledge of the melding process. In many cases modern spiritualist research has overlooked this basic and undeniable process which is essential to spiritual growth. There are two modern exceptions to this disregard of the facts of spiritual progression.

1. In his communication to Ruth Montgomery that later was published as a best-selling book, Bishop James Pike clearly indicates his awareness of the process.

2. The Myers work, conducted in England, used several capable psychics from all parts of the country. Each psychic was asked to reproduce a single sentence. They were told that their sentences would be put together in sequence with those of other psychics to make an unbiased, totally objective whole – a whole that would describe in detail the spiritual realms.[2]

Recent work by physicists indicates that atoms molecularize in the same way as spirits meld in their progression through the realms.

Looking again at Figure 7.1, you will note that we think there is another melding required before progression through what we call the 'last human gateway'. Though we have very few reports on these levels, we have hypothesized this melding from fragmentary reports and a sense of the 'rightness' of it. As you can see, it makes a repeatable pattern that is both logical and beautiful.

Summarizing the system – When a spirit passes into the spiritual realms at death, its first task is to synthesize its most recent earth plane experiences with its prior knowledge. If with guidance it can become selfless enough to meld and

[2]See T. C. Lethbridge, *Witches: Investigating an Ancient Religion.*

progress, it moves up into the cultural residence realms. If it cannot move up, it reincarnates to learn additional lessons through another lifetime. When an entity resident in the cultural realms wishes to progress, it must meld with entities from other cultural domains. If it cannot achieve this, it works as a guide and returns to the guidance level of the here-now. At the present time we have no idea what the ultimate melding involves. We can at this time see that each step implies the relinquishing of individuality, biases and egocentricity.

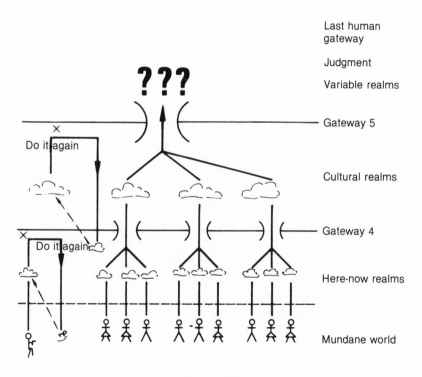

Figure 7.1
The Melding Process

Gateways

The age-old idea of gateways is helpful when discussing the movement of spirits in the realms. The astral here-now is the lowest realm, and it is approached through Gateway 1 (see Figure 6.1). There is no real division between the residence and guidance levels of this realm, even though the two levels are slightly different in function and ambience. Gateway 1 was easy and natural for you to get through; it is the gateway through which many proceed to obtain guidance during meditation. You either learned how to get through it by using the techniques we taught you earlier; or you got through it years ago, on your own. Whichever way you learned, you used certain techniques to force the gate: a key signal, a defined urgent necessity, a special state of protection.

Higher gateways are more difficult to pass. Apparently it is not usual for an incarnate spirit to go into the upper spiritual realms. Gateways 4 and 5 allow melded spirits to pass upwards and Guides and a select few incarnate spirits to pass in both directions.

The appearance of Gateway 4 is dependent on your own personality and cultural background. Analysis of many subjects has shown the following general culturally biased rules to be in force in respect to this gateway.

Culture	*Gateway Characteristics*

NORSE   The bridge of light (the Bifrost Bridge) is the way most people of Norse, Scandinavian or Germanic heritage visualize this gateway. Its guardian is a golden youth (Heimdal). Passing Gateway 4 leads to a residence area in which warrior characteristics are emphasized. Much loud boasting, feasting, carousing and clashes of arms can be heard. The area is forested with huge log halls and cabins in forest clearings. The melded discarnate spirits are larger than life.

CELTIC A spring, often flowing from a cave, symbolizes the gateway to Celts. Descent into the pool of water at the foot of the spring leads to a realm of castles inhabited by chivalrous knights and virtuous maidens (Camelot). Within the realm certain castles have great significance. Their walls are of vitrified stone or glass, and they have very complex maze-like approaches. Within the castles minor orgies occur; however, in the upper turrets of the castles there are far advanced guidance realms. The guardian of the gateway is a knight in black armour on a black horse. He is the personification of Death; if he lifts his visor you will see that he is only a skeleton.

JEWISH The gateway for the person of Jewish inheritance is difficult for anyone outside that heritage to understand. It is described as 'applied intelligence' (the 32nd path of the Sephiroth) and leads from femininity (or masculinity) to hermaphroditism. This is an obvious direct allusion to the melding process normally required for discarnate spirits to enter the upper realms. The rabbi in his teaching aspect is the guardian of this gate. The realm beyond the gate is noisy, with dancing and lots of sharp, bright music. Within the realm there is continuous argument and discussion. It seems that there are locations of abysmally poor-looking residences and other areas of extremely exotic housing. The spirits in the realm seem to ignore all of this.

LATIN This cultural group includes southern French, Italian, Spanish and several other peoples of Phoenician heritage distributed around the northern Mediterranean. For this group of people the symbol of the gateway is a rocky island shrouded in mist. Occasionally pillars of rock appear. The mist and the sea are a constant presence. The guardians of the gateway are a discarnate wailing voice and a boatman. Paying the boatman immediately transports you to the cultural level. Occasionally a subject has reported having to go by boat to the rocky island. The realm is a land of lotus-eaters. No one seems to do anything, but much telepathic communication goes on.

We have insufficient data from subjects to draw any real conclusions about conceptions of Gateway 4 for cultures other than those we have listed. Recently we have had a few reports of the Amerindian gateway, which seems to be a cool cave in a hot, dark desert scene where a howling coyote acts as the guardian.

We are told that the gate for Hindus is through the tantra yoga kundalini route, back through the egg and sperm to their original source. We need reports from more subjects on their perceptions of these other cultural gateways.

Once you start thinking about the gateways and the realms beyond them, you begin to see how ancient writings hint at and suggest them. These are the great archetypal stereotypes of each culture. Knowledge of the gateways has grown in recent years because of the increase in the numbers of people meditating and because of increased use of mind-expanding drugs. Every time a writer or other artist uses the archetypal stereotypes in his work, success is assured. Camelot is but the most recent example of such stereotype usage.

Knowledge of the gateways is in your subconscious mind, in what psychologists currently call your race memory. Once you bring it out, the meaning and the 'rightness' of the gateway and its symbology will become clear to you.

When you pass the gateway into your particular cultural realm, all other cultural realms become available to you. Think of the culture you want to visit, and you are there.

Think about an Amerindian tribe, and you will be able to enter its cultural residence realm. The realms seem to overlap; if you think of yourself at the intersection of the Norse and the Celtic realm, you will find yourself in a forested scene that may have stone castles or log huts. This is true for all the cultural domains. Since it is obviously true that in the physical world it is impossible for more than two or three realms to overlap each other, there is some space warping effect at work.

Passing the Gateway

Once you have formed in your mind characteristics of a given gateway that feel comfortable to you, the actual process of passing through the gateway is easy. All you have to do is find a quiet place in the appropriate guidance realm and concentrate briefly on the realms beyond the gateway and your reason for wanting to visit it. Then imagine yourself taking the appropriate steps; for example, walking across a Bridge of Light, and you will instantly arrive in the cultural realm. The occasional subject has reported that a Sage will take time to accompany him, provided that Sage is of the same cultural background as the subject.

All subjects, without exception, report that once they understand the meaning of the gateway, passing through it or over it is really extremely quick and simple. Many study groups on the earth plane make a huge production out of this natural, easy-to-accomplish experience. It is our opinion that the ability to pass a gateway should not be used as a criterion to assess spiritual development. Remembrance of gateway passages can be found in people who have had serious accidents, taken drugs or pursued other activities which are totally unrelated to the subject's level of spiritual development.

Characteristics Shared by the Cultural Domains

At first sight the various cultural domains bear little resemblance to each other. However, on longer acquaintance and after the analysis of visits to the realms of hundreds of subjects, a pattern of similarity does emerge. The first obvious similarity is that within the realms each culture produces an overdone stereotype of itself. It is as if each cultural attribute is over-emphasized to the point of comic-strip ridicule. Other similarities that have been noted are:

TIME
: To you the passage of time in the cultural domains is identical with the passage of time in the mundane. If you are in a cultural realm for 15 minutes, you will have been out of your body for 15 minutes. The time is the present. To date, no subjects report having been able to move backwards or forwards in time and then pass through a gateway into the spiritual realms. Apparently spiritual realms do not exist in past or future states. The concept of time that you have in your mundane thought patterns is not the concept of time that applies once you leave the lowest realm of the astral here-now. The only time that is existent in the upper spiritual realms is Now. Past history is forgotten and no realization of the future is apparent.

'NOW' IS EVERYTHING

SCENE
: The scenes you 'see' in cultural domains are created by the group consciousness of the spirits who dwell there. If you think yourself to an uninhabited area, you can create a scene to your own liking; that scene then seems to become a permanent part of the domain. If you are in an inhabited area and you see something that is out

of place, you can amend it by 'thinking it right'. However, you cannot easily create new areas to your liking within an existent populated area. The scene in a populated area is the result of the consensus reality of the spirits living there, and your changes can be made only if the consensus reality accepts them. Don't expect to be able to come in and rearrange everything in accordance with your will.

GUIDANCE Slightly offset from the cultural domain, and for convenience thought of as 'above' it, there is another guidance realm. The form of the guidance locations varies from one cultural domain to another. In the Celtic domain guidance seems to take place in the top rooms of towers. In the Norse domain it seems to take place while people sit on rocks on a seashore. In the Jewish domain it occurs in a more formal lecture-hall type setting. Just as in the guidance plane of the here-now, guidance counselling is conducted by more developed spirits who come down from a higher realm to do this type of work so as to further their own development.

Progression from the Guidance Level of a Cultural Realm

A ceremony is held where groups from different cultural domains meet and meld. This is another triple meld; that is, three spririts from three different cultures join and meld. Progression from the guidance realm requires that cultural differences be given up. In contemplating this scenario, philosophers conclude that cultural differences are more deep-rooted in human spirituality than are sexual differences, for the tri-sexual melding occurs before the cultural melding.

In this case melding is just as much a death experience as it is at the lower levels. It is the surrender of a huge block of learned attitudes. All those positive and negative biases towards people of other cultures have to be eliminated before the spirit is qualified to meld itself with spirits from 'strange' or 'foreign' backgrounds and cultures.

Gateway 5 – Beauty Itself

The gateway between the cultural domain at guidance level and the upper spirit realms we have called Gateway 5. This gateway is the same for all entities. The best description we can give of it is that it appears like an hourglass, wherein you must pass upwards through the narrow neck. The glass glows with its own pale violet translucent light. The light has sometimes been called 'beauty itself'. It does not radiate from any point; it has a clear all-pervading auric light. To get through the gate, you have to squeeze through the narrow neck of the hourglass without touching its sides; and you also know, without being told, that your auric light must exactly match that of the gateway. We have described the gateway as the neck of an hourglass, but this simplistic description does not do justice to the beauty and simplicity of the gate. In fact no words can describe it. Some of you are lucky enough to be able to recognize immediately what we are describing. The gateway is like a living consciousness. It needs no justification for its existence.

IT IS.
IT EXISTS BUT HAS NO BEING.

Simplistic Representation of the Spirit Realms

In the mundane world you are accustomed to the action/reaction concept. When you do something, something happens. Time passes. You think of the physical world as an ordered, sequential place. As soon as you move up into the spiritual realms, those concepts must be left behind. Time has no meaning in a place where Now is the only time that exists. Night and day also cease to exist in a world of ethereal light. Death changes its aspect. It is looked upon as a graduation from a lower level of existence to a higher.

DEATH IS A BEGINNING, NOT AN END.

Geographical scenery, possessions, all of these things you can have or change by using your own imagination.

Any representation of the realms of the spirit world must necessarily be incomplete and fall far short of a full explanation. Nevertheless, you need an outline if you are to have some idea of where you are. Such an outline is shown in Figure 7.2.

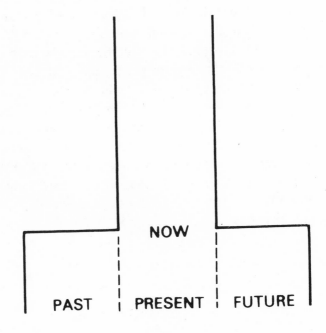

Figure 7.2
Simplistic Representation of the Spirit Realms

For convenience we have numbered the realms. We are well aware that there may be many more fine distinctions between the realms and that each level could be assigned a number. Many different numbering systems have been used throughout the ages to designate these levels of spirituality, but this is purely a matter of nomenclature and does not change the realms themselves.

Because the gateways are existent realms, they are included in the numbering. The Bridge of Light is a real bridge. The boatman on the river is a real boatman on a real river. The sketch to the left of the realm numbers in Figure 7.2 represents the change in the nature of Time as you travel upwards. In Realm 11 (mundane world) the past, the present and the future exist. At Realm 9 this concept continues in operation. But suddenly in Realm 8 only Now exists. The past and the future are meaningless and cannot be visited. Although the representation is two-dimensional, it must be remembered that the actual realms are multi-dimensional. For instance, Realm 6 is a seemingly endless continuum of widely different cultural domains. In Realm 6 you can extend the domains at will; therefore it is obvious there are no limits to the realms.

The Variable Realms

Gateway 5 leads to Realm 3. We call this the 'variable realm', and there are many reports of travel within it. The problem is that very few of the reports correlate with one another, as no consistent picture of the area can be constructed. What happens is that the thoughts and desires of each entity in the realm control its own environment. The realm is therefore so diverse that it defies understanding by our mundane senses. When you progress upwards in this realm, you finally come to an area of pale violet mistiness. Entities in this area are themselves clouds of pale violet. Occasionally these entity clouds change colour and leave the area. This seems to be the equivalent of an entity having to go back down to lower levels to gain more wisdom and control of its emotions. To progress from this realm, the entity must be totally in control of itself, have no undisciplined desires and be purged of all earthly emotions. The spirit has been cleansed of sexual and cultural bias and has learned that to develop it must reach back down the ladder of progress and help others upwards. Thus necessarily it must be a selfless, altruistic and unbiased entity. Most observers agree that there is guidance in this realm and that before leaving the realm an evaluation or judgment is made on the progress, and development of any given multi-melded spirit.

Judgment

Almost every ancient culture had some concept of judgment. Osiris who sits at the right hand of Ra, the Father Almighty, is there to 'judge the quick and the dead'. Mohammed serves a similar role in Islam; and Buddha judges the karmic record of the Buddhist. When judgment has been rendered and the melded spirit is allowed to progress, it goes through a final gateway out of the human development cycle. Where it goes has long been a subject of philosophical speculation.

In some philosophies this entity is believed to rejoin the Godhead; there is, however, some evidence that the spirit progresses to the bodies of more complex animals either on this planet or in other habitable spheres.

So far none of our researchers has become sufficiently developed to follow a cloud entity through Judgment and the last human gateway. Whether this is possible for an incarnate spirit is doubtful. Another hypothesis suggests that after passing the last human gateway, the variability experienced in Realm 3 increases, causing the least uncontrolled thought to produce swift and dramatic changes in the environment. That is one reason we call this realm the 'place we cannot think of', for every thought projected into the realm produces dramatic changes in it. If indeed this realm is God, then God becomes:

'THE BEGINNING WE CANNOT THINK OF'

for by thinking of or defining the realm, we change it. Each poor attempt we make to understand what lies beyond the last human gateway is in fact a doomed attempt to define

'THAT WHICH IS NOT DEFINABLE'.

Summary

Your concept of the realms will depend on your own background and cultural matrix. There are many other realms that you can visit and explore than we have cited, but we have no real documentation to describe them. Our descriptions of the realms are necessarily brief and biased by our own visits to them. When you visit them, you will be able to expand on the descriptions for yourself and place them in your own reality construct. Most of the books you read will give the personal view of a single observer. Do not be discouraged if each book gives a different view, or if none of them matches your own. Each author's view is from his own background and cultural matrix, not from yours.

Travelling in the spirit realms is easy and natural. From those realms you can get answers to all the mundane and spiritual questions you may ever have. Once you have visited the realms, you will find that you belong to an élite group, a group that has no need of priest, minister, or shaman.

CHAPTER 8

Liz and Bert Davis, the Couple Who Have Everything

'Look, Mummy! That's cruel.'

The little girl's high-pitched voice sounded above the hum of the diners in the castle's kitchen. She pulled at her mother's skirt until the slender blonde woman turned to look at the dog on its treadmill. By endlessly chasing a bone that hung from a string just before his nose, he was turning the spit in front of the open fire.

'He looks pretty happy to me,' the mother replied. 'See? See how plump he is? I'm sure they can't keep him at it very long.'

Even as they watched, an attendant gave the dog the bone he had been chasing and took the meat from the spit to a serving table. Its fragrance whetted the appetites of both mother and daughter. They made their way down the stone steps into the quarry-tiled coolness of the half-basement dining hall. After a moment's wait they spied an empty table and quickly made their way across the crowded room to it. Service was quick and efficient. They were just starting to eat when they were interrupted by a hesitant, 'Mind if I share your table, Ma'am?'

The gentle Welsh accent seemed incongruous from the tough-looking man who bent over her. Liz's first negative response died on her lips as she looked at the man more closely and noticed the bandages and sling that covered his right hand and arm. 'Why, ah, no. That's all right. Here, let me help you.'

Much to her daughter's amazement, Liz rose to help the young man with his tray. As she arranged his plate before him, brown eyes met blue and an indefinable shock passed between the two adults. 'Haven't I—?' 'Haven't we—?' They both laughed nervously and looked away as they simultaneously broke off the cliché question, realizing how stereotyped it sounded.

He recovered quickly. 'It's not a line,' he assured her.

'No, I know it's not. And I know where we met.'

'What's going on, Mummy?'

'Hush, Maggie. This young man and I know one another. Let's see. It's Bert, isn't it?'

Surprise flashed across Bert's face. 'Yes, but how—?' He thought for a moment. 'But damn it, I know you too. But what I remember – it can't have happened – can it?'

Liz blushed furiously and became very intent on her food. The young man was left with the sight of the top of her blonde head. He winked at Maggie, then turned to his own meal.

'What's the matter, Mummy?' Maggie tugged at her mother's sleeve.

Liz took a deep breath and looked up at both of them. 'I think this young man—'

'Bert', he interrupted.

'I think Bert and I—' she began again, 'shared a very unusual experience last night.'

'But you were at home with me last night!'

'I can't explain it,' Liz said with a trembling sigh. 'But I know how he injured his hand. I saw him go to the hospital, and I remember what happened after he had an anaesthetic. And not because he came into the chemist's, either.'

'And I do too,' Bert interrupted. 'And then we made l—'

Liz hastily laid her hand on his arm. He paused, noting the beginning of another blush and the erect nipples pushing through her summer blouse.

'You mean you met in a dream? Aw, you're both silly.'

'I don't think it's silly,' Bert said softly.

'I don't either,' Liz whispered back.

They spent a pleasant afternoon looking at all the historical houses and other exhibits at Fagan's Castle, the Welsh folk museum just outside Cardiff. Then the happy trio had high tea together. Liz invited Bert back to the small but well-kept apartment she and Maggie shared. Much to Maggie's embarrassment, Bert helped her mother bathe her. The two damp and tousled adults quickly got the little girl tucked in for the night.

They stood for a moment smiling at one another in the centre of the living room, knowing yet not believing what should come next. Liz broke the silence. She looked straight into his eyes. 'Let's go to bed.'

He was delighted and dismayed by her forthright invitation. 'Uh . . .'

'Remember last night?' She spoke softly, caressing his injured arm.

'But that didn't happen, did it?'

'You know it did, even if it wasn't physical.'

'I can't explain it . . . but does that matter?'

'We're not dreaming now! Let's see if we can be as good as we were then.'

That was enough for him. Quickly they both stripped off their clothes. He reached for her with his good hand.

She held him briefly at bay. 'Let's go to the bedroom.'

When it was over, they both slept deeply, but in their sleep they had another joint 'dream'. When they awoke they snuggled close. While she rested her blonde head on his dark, hairy chest he stroked her pale shoulder with the long, sensitive fingers of his uninjured hand.

'What's going on between us,' she wondered. 'Love at first sight?'

'I don't know,' he replied softly, 'and I don't want to ask for fear of breaking it. God, but it's wonderful!'

'Do you love me?' she murmured.

'I don't even know you!'

'But you're part of me!'

'I'm just not the sort of man who picks a girl up in the afternoon and screws her that evening. It — it's just not me. Yet with you ... Hell, yes, I love you! I want you. It's just like with the two halves of something.' He pushed her hair back from her face. They could both feel the passion rising in them again.

She pushed him gently away. 'Wait. I feel the same way about you. I know every little bit of you, even though ... You've never shopped at the chemist's in Tregarthen Street, have you? That's where I work.'

He shook his head.

'But I saw your accident yesterday. How you tried to save that Lascar[1].'

'How can this be? I've read stories in the Sunday rags about this sort of thing — but Jesus, I never thought it'd happen to me.'

'Me neither,' she responded.

'We ought to do something about it ... report it or something.'

'Tomorrow,' she sighed as they again let ecstasy grip them.

In the following days they desperately tried every avenue they knew, searching for a source of information that would explain the situation for them. The new young vicar of the chapel at which Bert sang was their first hope. Bert was content to sit back and let Liz explain what had happened to them.

'You see, Vicar, it was like this. Last Friday I had a tooth pulled in the afternoon after work. I had nitrous oxide. While I was under I dreamed — or I thought I dreamed — I was in the engine room of a ship at the dock. I saw this fellow push something out of the way as it swung towards the head of a Lascar. When he did it, his hand and arm got crushed against

[1]Lascar is the term for a Ceylonese deck hand.

the engine block. Then that night when I thought I was asleep in bed, I found myself in the hospital where they were working on Bert's arm; microsurgery, I think they call it. Anyway, Bert was there watching them work on him. And when he and I saw one another we ... um, ... ah, ... well, ... joined together. We kind of made love. It was wonderful.'

Bert helped Liz out of her embarrassment. 'You understand, Vicar, all this was like, we were dreaming, but I remember making love too.'

'Ah, yes, my boy, I understand. How did you meet one another?'

Liz took up the tale. 'Well, I was out at Fagan's Castle. Saturday was such a nice day. And Bert was there too, and we recognized one another. The bandage helped, I suppose. But we'd never met before except in that dream. Yet we immediately recognized one another. Neither of us could believe it, so we sort of spent the rest of the afternoon together, then ...' Liz drew back and turned to Bert for help.

'We've been living together ever since, and every time we make love we seem to dream of the same places afterwards. Sometimes we seem to join together in our dreams and it's like nothing either of us has experienced. It's ... just grand, is the only way I can say it.'

'Are you going to get married?'

'That part seems so unimportant somehow,' replied Liz without thinking.

The vicar was visibly shocked. 'What about the children?'

Liz and Bert looked at each other. A message passed. 'Well, Vicar, we think we'll be going now. Thank you for your time.'

'I didn't mean to criticize your lifestyle,' the vicar stammered.

'It's not that, Vicar. I'm sorry, but you just don't understand.'

They tried the Catholic priest, having heard that the

'Roman' way, as the Welsh call it, was more tolerant and knew more about the spiritual world. If anything, the priest was less helpful than had been the vicar. A couple of weeks later in a back room in an area down by the Cardiff docks, they found Swami Ras Bukti. After listening to their story he attempted to advise them of how to learn of his path to Nirvana. They were encouraged by his words, and came to a series of public meetings at which the Swami taught meditation and yoga techniques which he promised would allow everyone to gain the astral realms.

Liz and Bert found themselves turned off by the sick, lame and lazy pupils that the Swami seemed to have gathered around himself. The more they listened to the Swami, the stronger grew their conviction that he had never actually visited the realms he was describing. Moreover, they found that his techniques seemed to diminish the ease with which they had previously been able to do what they now called 'astral travelling' rather than 'dreaming'.

Liz and Bert went off the deep end. Every time they had a spare half hour they would go to bed together and make mechanical love, so that they could explore this new experience. Maggie was neglected, they didn't eat properly, the flat became a pigsty, but eventually they reached saturation. Liz could no longer have an orgasm on demand. Bert took the lack of 'love' on her part as a personal affront. In the cold light of dawn after a night of argument, they sat naked in the bed and looked at each other. 'Shall we split or marry?' Bert finally asked.

Liz regarded this cold proposal as a final insult. 'Why don't you fuck off?'

'All right.'

Two weeks later they met, again apparently by accident, in the restaurant at Fagan's Castle. 'We did it again, didn't we?' Bert said without preamble.

'Yes,' Liz sighed. 'I guess we're fated to be together.'

'That so bad?' he asked, reaching out to touch her.

She came willingly towards him. 'It's been lonely,' she confessed, 'and I've really missed astral travelling.'

'You sure it was just the travelling?' he teased.

'Oh, Bert, that too.'

'Come outside a minute,' he invited.

When she was seated on one of the old stone benches beneath an ancient pentagram, he proposed and she accepted. After the long kiss that sealed their bargain, she led him into one of the display halls. 'Bert, you read Welsh better than I do. Read what is says here on Dr Price's exhibit case.'

Bert read it to himself. As he read, he began to mumble. 'Jesus!' he finally exclaimed. 'Looks like this old boy knew all about it.'

'That's what I thought it said.'

'There's an address down here. Something to do with the history of medicine and a man you can contact. Got a pen?'

Liz handed Bert her neat chemist's notebook and a pencil. He carefully copied the address from the fine print in the museum case. Weeks later, after Liz and Bert were already married, they received a reply from the learned society to which she had carefully typed a letter. 'Would you kindly call Lord D— at Swansea—— and arrange a meeting,' was the full substance of the note. Bert was doubtful. 'A lord! What can he know about it?'

'Well, it can't hurt. And it's all we've got.'

Liz made the call. The lord was friendly and invited them to dinner.

'What should we wear?' Liz had the temerity to ask.

'Anything you like,' Lord D replied. 'It'll just be the family, Lady Evelyn and I. Maybe Sir Arnold will come. But it's you we're interested in. We want to hear everything you've been doing.'

'What did he mean by everything?' asked Bert suspiciously.

Liz elbowed him in the ribs. 'He sounded nice. Not at all la-de-da like you'd think. Just like my father used to sound. We don't have to tell him anything we don't want to.'

The following Saturday they had a pleasant run to Swansea in Bert's rebuilt Austin Seven, whose bright blue enamel bonnet and brass temperature gauge turned many heads on the road.

The Georgian house was set well back from the road in the hills overlooking Swansea. As they came up the drive two men in overalls were trying to unhook a tow-chain from the front of an Alvis Grey Ghost. As soon as they pulled up, Bert went over to lend a hand. When the chain was stowed away in the back of the Bentley, the plump and jovial elder of the two men wiped his forehead and said. 'Thanks. I'm Lord D. I imagine you're Bert.'

'Yes, your lordship.'

'Call me Harry. And this is Arnold,' said Lord D, introducing the tall thin man who now had grease in his beard. 'And I suppose this is Liz.'

'Yes, that's Liz.' Bert was more interested in the antique car. 'What's wrong with the Alvis?'

'She developed a knock on the way back from Pont-y-Prydd, so Arnold gave me a tow with his Bentley. Just spent two thousand quid on her coachwork over there. Bloody lovely job they did, but if the engine's gone bonkers it'll be money down the drain.'

'Will she run?'

'Oh, I can start her, all right. You know anything about 'em?'

'I know a bit about engines. I rebuilt mine.'

'Who did the coachwork on that one?'

'I did.'

Lord D noticed Liz standing isolated at the edge of the group. 'You go on into the house, m'dear,' commanded Harry. 'You'll find Evelyn out in the garden somewhere;

down with the herbs most probably.' As Liz left, the three men turned back to the ailing car.

Later that night after a light dinner Bert and Liz told their stories. The common interest in antique cars had broken any social barriers that might have prevented Bert from being candid with these aristocrats. In a similar manner, Lady Evelyn's knowledge of healing herbs had totally won Liz's admiration.

'Now, Bertrand, you and Elizabeth just tell us what you want to in your own words.' Harry invited. 'Arnold's going to run that tape machine of his.'

'That's if you don't mind,' Sir Arnold interrupted.

Bert and Liz were sufficiently comfortable to agree readily to the tape-recording of their experiences. Once more they told their story. This time their listeners nodded in agreement as they made each point.

'Bloody remarkable, it all happening spontaneously like that, don't you think so, my dear?' said Harry to Evelyn as Bert and Liz finished their recital.

'I've only got one other case that's anything near as good as this one,' commented Sir Arnold.

'Who are you?' asked Liz. 'What do you know that we don't?'

'Yes, I suppose it's our turn now,' Sir Arnold admitted. 'You want to tell 'em, Harry, or shall I?'

'Ah, you're better at the blather than I am. You do it. Let's get our drinks freshened up first, though.'

With many interruptions from Liz and Bert, Sir Arnold told them how knowledge of astral travel and astral projection had been preserved by the aristocracy in England during the witch-burning times and the various Christian suppressions. Only now, he disclosed, was this knowledge being recovered from family diaries and records by dedicated researchers. In addition, they were funding a small group to continue research into areas they were interested in, like astral travel and the use of herbs.

'Did you know the Queen's comin' down to open a hospital? One where they only use herbs?' Evelyn asked Liz.

'No, Ma'am.' Liz gaped. 'Is she really?'

'Yes, and I've got to find somebody to give her a bunch of herbs at the ceremony. Thirty-two different ones she wants in the bunch, all the ones they're going to use in the hospital. Would you like to do it, Elizabeth?'

Liz was literally struck dumb. 'I'd love to,' she finally stammered.

'When you two ladies have finished,' Sir Arnold sounded brusque, 'I want to know if our young friends will help in our researches.'

'What'll it involve?' Bert asked.

'Not much more than you've already been doing, Bertrand. We would like you to try to get out using some other techniques we're testing, and also we'd like you to narrow your explorations down and look for certain evidence to support our latest theories.'

'Um ... are these techniques, um, ah, sexual?' asked Liz hesitantly.

'No, m'dear; even I can do 'em,' joked Lord D.

'Will we be able to get out without making love?' she persisted.

'Most people can,' Sir Arnold replied.

Liz sighed her relief. 'I think that'll make things a lot easier, don't you, Bert?'

'Yes, I think so, darling. Just doing "it" so as to get out makes it somehow boring.'

'You don't realize how lucky you are, young man,' Lady Evelyn chided him. 'In my young day we couldn't officially use sex. It was very difficult for us to get out the first time. Then too, by using sex for something more than personal gratification you're really way ahead of the poor dears out there who don't understand and copulate like animals.'

It was past midnight when Liz and Bert finally made their farewells to their new friends. Liz carried with her a whole set of instructions from Sir Arnold. She had promised to stay in contact with him on the mundane level and she had also promised to attempt to find him in the astral.

Freeing their researches from the need for constant orgasms brought balance and serenity back into Liz and Bert's life. Almost every night found them exploring different astral realms. They had immediate success with the twilight-zone system, although occasionally Bert was too tired from his work and fell deeply asleep before they were able to project together. On the first few occasions when this happened, Liz projected herself and then told Bert of it in the morning. Bert, however, did not like her travelling alone. Whether through reasons of his own jealousy or through concern for her safety, he became extremely emotional when she astral travelled without him. Liz therefore stopped this practice and thus avoided the marital problems that many of the Institute's researchers encountered when one of a couple found it easy to astral travel and the other did not.

Lord D and Lady Evelyn really looked upon Elizabeth and Bertrand more as their children than as fellow researchers. At the party after the presentation of herbs from one Elizabeth to another, Harry made Bert, as he now called him, a rather startling offer. 'We have a bit of property back in the hills; got an old farmhouse on it and a bloody fine barn. How'd you like to go into the business of fixing antique car engines? I'll stake you while you fix the Alvis. I've got dozens of friends who really need the same kind of service from somebody they can trust.'

'You been listening in on Liz and me talking?' Bert demanded.

'No! You know we wouldn't do that.'

'Well, it's another one of those "coincidences", I suppose,' Bert reflected. 'But Liz and I were talking about having to get out of town 'cause our lives have changed so much that the town just jangles our nerves and we can't repaint the flat the way we want to. The landlord just won't have it. Let me take Liz out to this place of yours; then we'll let you know. Okay? I really am grateful, though, to your lordship.'

'Harry,' the older man amended. 'I know you're a Christian, Bert,' he continued, 'but we belong to a group we like to think of as seekers. Maybe we were witches in the old days; I dunno. But if we don't all stick together then who can?'

Years have gone by since that conversation. Liz and Bert now own a neat farmhouse with a thriving antique car restoration business in the barn. Lord D has passed into Side. Recently he made his last visit to Liz and Bert on the astral.

The Wise Computer

Liz, Bert and Maggie exist only in the statistical memory of an English computer. They were invented to avoid boring you with collections of dull statistics and their analysis. They are the mean, within one standard deviation, of the students and researchers who took part in the English portion of the decade-long experiment in astral travel conducted by the Canterbury Institute.

Elizabeth (Liz) Mary Davis née Nesbitt

Born	3 April 1951
Height	5 feet 7 inches
Weight	9 stone 1 pound (127 pounds)
Complexion	Fair (blue-eyed blonde)
Marriages	first married at 18; marriage lasted 4 years. Has one daughter as result of this marriage; now in second marriage
Work	Chemist (pharmacist)

Sidney Bertrand (Bert) Davis

Born	10 November 1947
Height	6 feet 1 inch
Weight	14 stone 6 pounds (202 pounds)
Complexion	Swarthy
Marriages	after many 'liaisons' this is his first permanent relationship
Work	Marine diesel mechanic

Certain patterns of lifestyle emerged from the compiled statistics of those who were successful astral travellers and persisted with the research.

EXPERIENCE	Prior spontaneous astral travel had been experienced by almost all of the participants. In many cases this had been induced either through an accident or as a result of the use of anaesthetics or, in a small percentage of cases, by hallucinogenic drugs.
LIFESTYLE	All the participants, without exception, made dramatic changes in their way of living. The changes ranged from merely moving closer to the country to changing nations. In most cases the interiors of their dwellings were repainted in light pastels. They threw away many possessions that they came to feel were irrelevant, and in many cases made major changes in dietary habits. These changes took place over many months as they progressed in their knowledge of the astral realms.
OBSESSION	In many cases obsessive behaviour

occurred when researchers first realized they could trip out into the astral. Temporarily many seemed to abandon the physical world for that of the astral. These obsessions often resulted in marital and job-related problems.

SEX

Some spontaneous astral travel resulted from mutual orgasms on the part of young couples. In cases where they realized what had happened, this resulted in a violent increase in sexual activity. This level of sexual activity dropped back to accepted norms or even below accepted norms when they began to participate in an orderly development programme. The employment of sex as a means rather than an end in itself was an entirely new concept to them, and seemed to be very beneficial to most participants.

RELIGION

The fact that most clergymen were unable to explain the occurrences that concerned the astral travellers meant that the majority turned away from their hereditary religion, feeling it was a sham. Because of peer group pressure most stayed with their churches, though they only attended in a perfunctory way and rarely spoke to their minister. Years later they often returned to their churches to help those with less awareness.

ARISTOCRACY

The British aristocracy and a small élite group of people holding several advanced degrees led in all the research efforts. In the

United States' effort, the records show that people with advanced degrees and high IQ dominated the work.

SALVAGE In case after case, participants reported a new and lively interest in antiques and in the salvaging of old houses, cars, graveyards and many other discarded and overlooked objects.

GROUP ACTIVITY When participants were introduced to one another, they tended to stay together, often forming working groups or extended families within the existent cultural matrix. These extended families crossed all social barriers and often included people of widely different cultural backgrounds. Many small theatre groups, historic societies and historically orientated hobby groups owe their formation to this tendency.

SOCIAL VALUES The researchers found that non-astral travellers valued things like marriage that to the researchers were very secondary and unimportant. In some ways the researchers became outcasts from their own society, but they ignored the ostracism because they found strength and companionship from the astral.

It is apparent that many of the common tendencies of the participants are outward manifestations of the inner spiritual changes taking place. When they began to travel on the astral, the participants experienced internal value changes which resulted in lifestyle changes and friendship with others who had similar value sets. These value sets were not merely superficial or short-lived fads. They became a permanent part of the participants' character.

CHAPTER 9
The Secrets of the Grimoires

Ancient writings often contain clues revealing that the writers were fully conversant with the structure of the astral realms. Ancient civilizations took far more time to explore non-physical reality than most people do currently, and they did not have the artificial restraints placed on them by priestly leaders which came into vogue with the establishment of city-states and religious hierarchies. In the western world, people are well aware of the strictures that church leaders placed on spiritual exploration. What is not commonly realized is that the same strictures against exploration of the realms were enforced on the laity in such cultures as the Egyptian and the Hindu. It is clear that when a priestly class is established in a culture, it has a vested interest in forbidding exploration, for if lay people are allowed to explore the realms, the priestly class is no longer needed. Answers to philosophical and mundane questions can be obtained by the people without the need of a priestly middleman. So that they can exert the maximum influence, trained priests of any large religious body are necessarily taught to resist the laity's personal exploration of the astral. If need be, they strictly forbid such exploration, adjuring it as 'the Devil's work'.

In every walk of life and in every age there will be many people to whom this stricture is meaningless, for they have already gone beyond a priest-structured sterile concept of reality. These are the true mystics, not pseudo-mystics produced by delving into a bottle (whether it be of alcohol or pills). For them, the true mystics, the mystical reality is an absolute necessity. Talking about it to a trained priest leads to frustration and disappointment, for the mystic finds himself speaking in terms unable to be comprehended by one who has not had similar experiences. Mystical writings of many cultures go beyond and behind the dogma of priests in an attempt to satisfy the needs of these individuals.

Egyptian Mysticism

There is a tendency to think that Egyptian religious thought sprang to life in full flower with the earliest pharaohs some 6,000 years ago. This of course is not true. The system developed as Egypt went from tribalism through the city-state stage and finally into the dynastic stage. We are indeed extremely fortunate that the climate of Egypt preserved so many documents containing information about the astral realms and about Egyptian thoughts on reality, though the earliest records are lost. The records that remain are those that were preserved in the tombs of the great pharaohs and of the nobles. It is clear from review of the earliest pharaonic records that ideas of a less sophisticated cosmology and of city or village gods are still present in the later religion. Some difficulty exists in sorting out ideas involved with city-god concepts from those passages that show understanding of the complete spiritual system.

One other problem in deciphering the real beliefs from those beliefs to which they paid only lip service is that, as with all people, they had a tendency to retain the traditional rituals for many centuries beyond the time at which they had outgrown the beliefs underlying the old rituals. This is particularly notable in the change from belief in resurrection of a corruptible body to reincarnation of the spirit. This change occurred early in Egyptian thinking, only 2,000 years or so after the date of the first mummy – yet they continued to mummify their dead. Sir W. Budge comments specifically on this tendency to preserve outdated modes and religious practices.[1]

There were ignorant people in Egypt who, no doubt, believed in the resurrection of the corruptible body, and who imagined that the new life would be, after all, something very much like a continuation of that which they were living in this world; but the Egyptian who followed the teaching of his sacred writings knew that such beliefs were not consistent with the views of their priests and of educated people in general. Already in the Vth dynasty, about B.C. 3400, it is stated definitely:
> The soul to heaven, the body to earth . . .

In the first 2,000 years of Christianity the belief in resurrection of the corruptible body was strongly held. Now, however, the situation is beginning to parallel that in Egypt. Hopefully, if Christianity lasts another 4,000 years, understanding of reincarnation will come back to the world – after a lapse of a mere 6,000 years.

Understanding Egyptian Concepts of the Astral Planes

The Rosetta Stone was a stone of destiny in that it broke the code of the hieroglyphics; but it is also a very limited translation device, for it gives a mechanistic, literal translation of the pictograms. It is important to understand that the Egyptian written language is a series of pictures not translatable in a fixed manner. Each pictogram can be looked upon as a group of letters or even a full word. What that word actually means is dependent on the context and on the understanding of the pictogram. In spiritual matters this is extremely subjective and dependent on the reality of the person doing the translation. When 'God' is referred to as 'Him', it is often because the tran slator was unconsciously orientated to a male god because of his cultural matrix. The pictogram certainly does not show the gender of the Ultimate Diety, for it was always held that the

[1]*Egyptian Religion* published by Dell.

Ultimate Deity could not be depicted. In such phrases as 'He is undefinable', 'He cannot be figured in stone', 'He is God the son of God', the gender has been arbitrarily assigned. In a land where equality between the sexes was an axiom that was taken for granted, it is unlikely that the Ultimate Deity was always regarded as male – yet 'It' is always translated as male.

With these facts in mind, it is easy to see how the translation of a pictogram representing 'the primeval void' can be taken in many ways. The scholarly translators were mainly Christians. To expect them to be able to understand the subtleties of the astral realms is unrealistic. Yet even through the dimming haze of the centuries and the biases of the translators, we can still perceive a complete and accurate description of the astral realms in the various books of the dead taken from papyri, coffin texts and tomb murals.

Egyptian Beliefs

Some interesting Egyptian beliefs that parallel the knowledge you can gain from the astral realms are:

1. The Supreme Being – Several texts describe It as being impossible to imagine. 'His face cannot be imagined or depicted.' It is described variously as 'self-existent strength', 'the active power which creates in regular recurrence', 'the power to renew'. It is also allowed to speak of Itself as 'the Creator of the primeval void' and to say such things as, 'I evolved the evolving of evolution.'

2. The parts of an entity – As the Egyptians learned more about the astral, they went through a series of changes in their thinking about the constituent parts of a being. In the texts eight different parts are readily identified, but in later thinking they can be reduced to three. Again confusion

exists in the nomenclature because as the Egyptians reduced the number of the constituent parts from eight to three, they retained the attributes of some of the discarded parts in the ones they kept. Reviewing these entity parts:

KA   The etheric double of a person remains attached to the body even after death. It has some freedom of movement, but is attached by a subtle cord. Because the Egyptians knew that no matter how well they mummified a body it would still corrupt, they often arranged for a Ka residence in a tomb in the shape of a statue which was an exact replica of the dead person.

BA   The sublime spirit or soul was contained within the Ka, yet it is totally separable. It is the immortal imperishable part of a person. In the papyri it is shown as a human-headed hawk that can fly where it will. It often returns to visit the Ka after death.

KHU   The celestial being. When the Ba has been purified and lives with the gods, the Khu comes into its own. It is the being that lives on in the shape of a perfected replica of the earth-plane shell.

SEKHEM   The vital force or 'strength personified'. This was looked upon as the life force, the force that made something live, and it was originally considered to be different, and separate from, the preceding four. The Sekhem was also considered to be the power that allowed one to have mastery over something.

KHAIBIT   The shadow. In some ways this signified the dark side of a being, but in others it was a concept of the presence of the spirit being felt as a shadow.

REN   The name. This is the secret name, the name of

power. It was one of the most important constituent parts of an individual. If you could
eliminate a person's name from all records, he
himself would be eliminated. Control of the person
was yours once you learned the secret name, for it
told you the innermost secrets of an entity's soul.

Gateways

The Egyptians had a highly developed concept of gateways
between realms. The books of the dead describe not only the
gates themselves, but also the manner in which the entering
soul should ask for and receive entrance. These are often
shown in question-and-answer format and sometimes as
personal confessions. The confession required of a person to
gain admission to the next level may run to many verses. One
of the shorter versions is:

> I have not cursed Thee nor taken Thy name in vain.
> I have obeyed the laws of man.
> I have not borne false witness.
> I have not stolen, nor have I been deceitful.
> I have put out new cakes and ale so that a Ka may feed.
> I have not made any afraid.
> I come in peace.

'I have not made any afraid.' If this single precept were in
force today and people really believed, as did the Egyptians,
that it was a required prerequisite for admission to heaven . . .
It's an awesome thought.

The equivalent to Gateway 4 was depicted as the god
Hapi. Occasionally Hapi appears as two gods, one wearing a
papyrus and one a lotus head-dress. At other times he appears
as 'the One', being an entity of larger than usual size with
both male and female attributes. Significantly enough, at
Hapi gates the god appears as two gods on one side of the

gate and one god on the other. Much symbolism depicts the joining together of the two halves of Egypt. The black Nubian joins with the Lower Delta person. Throughout all this the River of Life, the Nile, brings all together. The Egyptian symbolism of melding is easily understood by those who have visited the astral, yet not one Egyptologist has ever truly explained the gates of Hapi.

According to the translators, the Egyptian concept of Gateway 5 is a gate of blue fire through which the applicant must pass to be judged by Osiris.

Judgment

The Egyptians recognized that they would be judged many times as they progressed upwards. In scenes on some papyri we see the heart being weighed against the man. This concept is apparently a recognition that to progress the spirit must balance with the body. In our terminology, the 'I' and the 'Me' must be in harmony.

The ultimate judgment is the weighing of the heart against the Feather of Truth. A perfect balance is required. The scene is always populated with many aspects of the deity, all of whom are present in their anthropomorphic state to make sure that the weighing is fair. Once the entity passes this evaluation, his Khu can rejoin the gods and live forever in the unknown realm.

Not content with merely living in this unknown realm, the entity tries to progress until it actually becomes an inseparable part of the Divinity. To attain this blessed state, the entity beatifies each part of itself in turn, first identifying each limb with a lower god and then identifying them with the Unknown. The last saying the entity repeats is typically: 'There is no member of my body which is not a member of the God. I am Thoth by night and Ra by day.'

Egyptian Astral Residence Planes

Confusion exists both in understanding and in separating the three main astral residence realms in the Egyptian cosmology. The three areas are:

1. *The Tuat*, sometimes called the Duart. This can most easily be compared to the astral here-now. It was conceived as being an exact replica of Egypt that existed over the western horizon. It was approached either at night by the light of the moon by water, or on the high road by land in the sun, an obvious reference to the fact that both the male and the female paths allowed access.

2. *Sekhet Aaru* – the land of reeds. This is an astral cultural residence plane. It has the same larger-than-life characteristics that we find today in the cultural realms. For a farmer it is described as a 'large, well-kept, well-stocked homestead situated close to the mother of life, the Nile'. It is a perfect farm, and it is noted that no animals, 'neither fish nor serpents nor worms of any kind whatsoever' exist there. The entities are oversized, being 'seven cubits high'. The perfect white wheat is said to grow 'three cubits and more'.

3. *The Maat* – This is the realm approached through the gate of blue fire. Conceded to be far to the east of Egypt, it is the realm in which one is eventually brought before Osiris for judgment. A description of the floor of the Maat is common to many papyri: 'A place where neither a pig nor any other animal has ever trod,' showing again the Egyptians' clear understanding that there are no animals on the astral.

A Tentative Egyptian Cosmology Construct

From our very limited comprehension of the Egyptian world-view, we can put down what we know and compare it with our modern perceptions. Such a comparison is shown in Table 9.1. The correlation is obvious and shows that truth is truth, no matter in what age it is found or in what form it comes to us.

Modern Name	Egyptian	Realm
The Place We Cannot Think Of	The One	0
The Last Human Gateway		1
Judgment (Evaluation)	Judgment of Osiris	2
The Variable Realms	The Maat	3
Gateway 5	Gate of Fire	4
Cultural Domain Guidance		5
Cultural Domain Residence	Sekhet Aaru	6
Gateway 4	Gate of Hapi	7
Here-Now Guidance		8
Here-Now Residence	The Tuat	9
Gateway 1	Male/Female Paths	10
Mundane World	Egypt	11

Table 9.1
Correlation between Egyptian and Modern Realms

An Indian Cosmology

The eastern holy books, although not written until well after Egypt's Golden Age, date from the same period. It is quite amazing that the Hindu cosmology also exactly correlates to both modern and ancient fact, especially when it is realized that the cosmology was transmitted verbally for many centuries. In order to ensure the transmission of the system, a simple metaphor was developed relying on the idea of 'as above, so below'. That is, the world as we perceive it on the mundane plane is a miniature representation, a microcosm, of the total cosmic and astral macrocosm. A simple extension of this idea is to see the human body as a microcosm of the world.

The climb towards awareness and self-realization is then conceived as the path of two currents or serpents, one male, one female, climbing through the body and at certain specific points meeting and melding. The mundane world is compared to the lowest point of a seated figure; that is, the anus. As each plane of realization is reached, it is considered that the serpents have passed and ignited an area in the body called a cakra (colloquial: chakra). Figure 9.1 shows a seated entity with the two intertwining currents climbing through the body towards the ultimate awareness where, in an instant of brilliant awareness, they will be made one with the consciousness. In this case the consciousness is the microcosmic

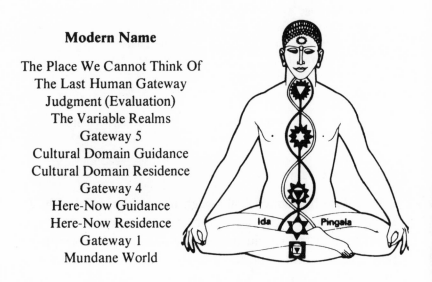

Modern Name

The Place We Cannot Think Of
The Last Human Gateway
Judgment (Evaluation)
The Variable Realms
Gateway 5
Cultural Domain Guidance
Cultural Domain Residence
Gateway 4
Here-Now Guidance
Here-Now Residence
Gateway 1
Mundane World

Figure 9.1
Correlation between Microcosm and Modern Realms

representation of the One unknowable indefinable overseeing God. This is an interesting concept in that it is obviously very difficult for a graven image to be made of such an idea as Consciousness or Awareness. If we cannot make a graven image of the microcosmic representation of the One, how, the Swami asks, can you hope to make a representation of the Ultimate Deity?

Following the path of the currents from the anal cakra, we first reach the genitalia. The here-now astral realm still retains sexuality. Only after passing the genitalia do the currents meld before they proceed upwards.

The cultural realms are represented on two levels. The 'gut feel' for your culture is represented by the solar plexus cakra. This gut feel has to be suppressed before you can bring into control the heart-level cakra, which represents the life force of a culture in a purer sense. After melding, we come to the throat cakra, which is Truth, the gateway through which Truth is communicated and through which you are judged. Passing this level leads the spirit to melding with the awareness, i.e., returning to meld with the Ultimate Deity.

The Judaic Mystical Perception

The Jewish mystical literature is undoubtedly the most rich in allegory of those that have come down to us from the ancient world. The Kabbalah (the Tradition) is the collective term for all this literature. It is dramatically different from rabbinical Jewish thought. Jehovah is no longer God Almighty; instead he is subordinate to the Unknowable God, the En-Sof.

The Tree of Lights

A cross-cultural commonality between the Kabbalah and western cultures is the Tree of Lights, the Sephiroth. This is the flowering tree that signifies the growth of understanding.

It is also the Christmas tree and the Freedom Tree that the colonists lit on Boston Common. Climbing the tree symbolizes climbing up through the spiritual realms.

Because of the same translation and interpretational differences that occur with the Egyptian cosmology, some of the names given to the parts of the Sephiroth seem unusual; however, when you understand the original meanings of the names you can see how well synchronized the system is with current thought.

VICTORY	This represents victory over earthly mundane cares and appetites. Symbolically it is often thought of as the day of the creation of the sun and the moon, those heavenly bodies that lift men's eyes away from earthly problems.
GLORY	The Jews did not divide the here-now plane into two because there is no real barrier between the guidance and residence realms. Glory is also called Majesty, and perhaps this better symbolizes the here-now astral planes.
BEAUTY	This is one of the most important sephirothic lights. Whole treatises have been written on it. The major gateway between the Greater and the Lesser, Beauty, is always described as bisexual. This is a clear indication that the ancients recognized the sexual melding required before discarnate entities can proceed through the gate.
LOVE (MERCY)	Here again is a single description of realms we nowadays divide into two. The Sephiroth considers this light to be the expansion of the

will, and of course that correlates well with the fact that in these realms an individual spirit can create its own environment. The will here is everything, for by use of will all is accomplished.

Comparing the names of the lights of the Sephiroth (as shown in Table 9.2) with the modern names we have given the astral realms shows an immediate correlation between ancient and modern views of the spiritual world.

Modern Name	Sephiroth Name	Realm
The Place We Cannot Think Of	Crown	0
The Last Human Gateway		1
Judgment (Evaluation)	Understanding	2
The Variable Realms	Wisdom	3
Gateway 5	Justice (Power)	4
Cultural Domain Guidance	Love (Mercy)	5
Cultural Domain Residence		6
Gateway 4	Beauty	7
Here-Now Guidance	Glory	8
Here-Now Residence		9
Gateway 1	Victory	10
Mundane World	Foundation	11
	Kingdom	

Table 9.2

Correlation between Sephiroth and Modern Realms

One of the most important teachings contained in the Sephiroth is that each light is connected to other lights by a series of paths. Learning how to work these paths is a major part of the kabbalist's training. A familiarity with the paths is of use to an astral traveller; however, the important part of this knowledge is that you can travel directly from one realm to another. You do not have to climb your tree progressively; instead you can move from the mundane to any realm you wish, provided only that you can visualize in detail the realm you wish to visit. For this reason we recommend that in your first trips into the astral spirit realms you explore in an orderly, progressive way, starting at the lowest and proceeding upwards in sequence; otherwise you may become confused and not know what realm you are in.

Guideposts in the Tarot

Another excellent guide to the spirit realms is contained in the ancient divinatory cards called the tarot.

Just as in the case of the Sephiroth and other ancient traditions, the names of the cards are not necessarily indicative of the real symbology. Fortunately, in the case of the cards we do have actual pictures to go along with the names.[2] Unfortunately, the order of the cards has been rectified several times in recent years, apparently by people who had no idea of the progressive nature of the astral realms. The general sequence has been retained, but some of the cards have been placed out of order by scholars who could not perceive the sequence of the ideas expressed in them.

THE HANGED MAN   The divinatory meaning of the Hanged Man has always been surrender to the will of a higher being and the upsetting of mundane ways of thought. Looking at the symbology of the card, you see the aura around the head of the man; this reveals that the original artist knew auras became visible after the gateway was passed.

DEATH AND THE DEVIL   Obviously death represents a gateway. The card itself shows the black knight on his horse (cf. the Celtic symbology).

[2]We recommend you use a tarot deck based on the 'Waite' system.

The visor is raised, showing clearly that a skeleton inhabits the armour. Finding the devil at this level is somewhat unusual, until you examine the card. Thereon you find a male and a female chained together, showing the sexual melding that goes on before the discarnate can pass the gate. The beast shown on the card is made up of pieces of many animals, again showing that the ancients knew of the melding process.

TEMPERANCE

Although the card is called Temperance, it shows the juxtaposition of a wilderness and a tended garden. The figure on the card is mixing two different waters, showing again the mixing of cultures in these astral realms.

Table 9.3 tabulates the cards against the astral realms.

Modern Name	Tarot Card	Realm
The Place We Cannot Think of	The Fool	0
The Last Human Gateway	The World	1
Judgment (Evaluation)	Judgment	2
The Variable Realms	Sun Moon & Star	3
Gateway 5	The Tower	4
Cultural Domain Guidance	Temperance	5
Cultural Domain Residence		6
Gateway 4	Death & The Devil	7
Here-Now Guidance	Justice	8
Here-Now Residence		9
Gateway 1	The Hanged Man	10
Mundane World	Cards 1 to 10	11

Table 9.3
Correlation between Tarot and Modern Realms

How Other Systems Correspond

Within the space limitations of these pages we cannot explore all ancient cultures; some that you may wish to explore on your own include:

1. *Central American* – These cultures are generally over-looked by seekers after spiritual knowledge. It is true that they are explored by pyramid- and time-enthusiasts, but they also contain instructions on occult matters. Recent Russian translations of the Mayan codices reveal a huge storehouse of unexplored astral wisdom.

2. *Oriental* – Many people are turned off by the convoluted sayings of ancient Oriental philosophers. These sayings become crystal clear, however, to anyone who has experience in the astral. The writings of Lao Tse are typical of the literature and are rich in instructions for astral travel to those who can contemplate them. The meditative training and the contemplation of single objects help the seeker to define urgent necessities and gateways. This singleness of thought is most necessary in astral work.

3. *Celtic* – Although only fragments of a larger picture, the ancient Celtic writings speak continually of people whose playground was the astral here-now. The shape-changing, the tasks set, the land under the hill, are all direct references to travel into the astral realms and long periods spent there. For the Celts, communication between many realities was obviously an everyday occurrence. Even today, time runs far slower for the Celts than it does in the rest of the world.

4. *Norse* – Heroic tales of Norsemen with their multi-layer Valhalla and the ever-present overwatching spiritual realm of the Aesir are the most explicit descriptions of the astral

spiritual realms of any ancient literature. It's all there for you to read and understand. As with all good literature of this type, it can be understood and enjoyed on two levels: the adventure story of the gods against the giants, and the underlying description of the astral realms.

5. *African* – Although books on these cultures contain little material on the astral, still most people from the cultures can speak of the spiritual realms without hesitation. As with the Celts, for a person of African heritage the barrier between the astral and the mundane is very thin and easily penetrated. Much information on the astral can be obtained merely by holding a conversation with one of the elders of any African heritage group, provided only that the elder has not been thoroughly brainwashed into an alien religious framework.

Summary

In using the ancient writings as a guide to the astral realms, especially those that have been translated into modern idiom or have commentaries with them, you should be aware of two problems:

1. The symbols that are brought to mind by the language of the ancient writings have a different meaning for you in your twentieth-century reality than they did in ancient time. Just as the symbols in dream symbology are personal to the observer and his reality, so the symbols of the ancients are different from our symbols of today.

2. Translators and commentators – Many of these people are highly trained scholars. They can perfectly translate words in a literal sense; however, if they have never astral travelled they have no knowledge of what they are trying

to convey. In the past, wars have been fought over the translation of modern languages; a well-known case was the translation of a treaty from French into English. How much more likely are errors to be introduced when the translator has no knowledge of the realm he is describing and when the language is from a long-dead culture or written in pictograms rather than the Roman alphabet.

There are many other keys to the realms in other disciplines that have cross-cultural significance. Music, numbers, astrology, myth and many other arts contain such clues. Once you have visited the realms, you will recognize the underlying meaning of many things that seemed earlier to have only one level of interpretation.

Although the nomenclature and the perception of reality from culture to culture, from age to age, may vary, the astral realms are obviously unvarying.

CHAPTER 10
Healing and Helping with Astral Projection

Your world-view should now be different from that of most people you meet in your daily round. This is because through your astral projections you can gain serenity and confidence in the future and lose all fear of what others think of you. Reflect for a moment with us. You meet a charming person who seems to like you; yet a friend says that this person actually sneers at you behind your back. A very quick astral trip, and you can determine who is telling the truth and the reasons behind the conflicting stories.

YOU KNOW. YOU ARE SURE.

Table 10.1 compares your new characteristics ·with the characteristics of a person who has no knowledge of astral projection.

Your Attributes	*Their Symptoms*
Trust	Distrust
Assurance	Doubt
Confidence	Fear
Tranquillity	Anxiety-Worry
Receptivity	Prejudice

Table 10.1
The New/Old You

To help others, you must have the characteristics shown in the left-hand column of Table 10.1. Without them, it is indeed a case of the blind leading the blind.

Before you begin to help others, you must be in full command of your own body and resources. Everything we say in the next few pages about helping yourself can be applied to helping others, and vice versa.

The Spirit and the Body

When 'I' and 'Me' are together in your body, each affects the other. A 'regular doctor', what we shall call an RD, cares for 'Me'. A psychiatrist or a priest attempts to care for 'I'. The general terms used in the mundane world for 'I' and 'Me' in connection with healing are 'psyche' for 'I' and 'somatic' for 'Me'. It is gradually being recognized that every illness affects both the psyche and the somatic, and that the root cause of an illness is often in the psyche, leading to a 'psychosomatic' illness. In Chapter 2 we told you to find a pool of still, darkened water in which you could view your own 'I', and that when you viewed your 'I' you might find things you disliked about 'I's' appearance. We told you then to think pleasant, positive thoughts and to see how this changed 'I's' appearance. Retention of these pleasant-making thoughts helps you in the mundane world.

This is a quick-fix approach. Most people can't go around all day every day thinking pleasant, happy thoughts. The permanent fix is to change your lifestyle so that 'I's' appearance is permanently changed. You can do this by making minor changes in your lifestyle, settling into them, and then viewing their effect in your psychic mirror. This is also the process to use in helping another person.

Let us say when you are viewing 'I', instead of a pleasant white aura around you, you notice that you have an aura suffused with a particular colour. Table 10.2 shows the generally accepted meaning of these colours and the balancing colours that you can bring into your mundane life to neutralize those excessive energies to improve your physical and emotional health.

Excess Colour	Meaning	Balancing Colour
Black	Death	White
Red	Anger	Turquoise
Blue	Cold Personality	Yellow
Green	Money or Sex	Violet
Yellow	Mental Control	Blue
Violet	Too Spiritual	Green
Turquoise	Lustful	Red

Table 10.2
Getting Excessive Colour into Balance

Bringing these balancing colours into 'Me's' life is extremely simple. All you have to do is wear clothing, or paint a room, or buy a car, of the colour you need; this will automatically bring the balancing colour into your life and you will find that 'I's' appearance in your psychic mirror will gradually improve.[1]

As explained in the books referenced in the footnote, these energies are obtainable not only from coloured objects; they are also given off by various materials and amulets. The emotional energies can also be generated by chanting and during occult rituals. This requires that the high priest or occultist key into the correct colour and other symbology so that he generates energy of the correct emotional content. In old books called 'grimoires' extensive directions are often given regarding ways to achieve such energy tuning. The School of Wicca teaches a course in Practical Sorcery; in that course too we give detailed instruction in the art of raising and directing tuned energies. If yours are really way out of balance, we suggest you take the course so you can more effectively help yourself.

[1]For more information on balancing the energies in your life, see *A Witch's Grimoire of Ancient Omens, Portents, Talismans, Amulets, and Charms* or *Meta-Psychometry: Key to Power and Abundance* both by Frost and Frost, and both available through the School.

Healing Your Own Psyche

An easy way to restore the energies lacking in your aura is to construct a small bag of natural linen to serve as a 'medicine bag'. This medicine bag is to be worn each day hung around your neck or from your belt. Table 10.3 shows the items you should place in the bag to cure an imbalance of the specified colour.

Balancing Colour	Herb	Flower	Stone	Scented Object	Metal
Nail clipping or hair					
White	Poppy	Night-scented Stock	Pearl	White Sandalwood	Silver
Turquoise	Sweet Basil	Cactus	Turquoise	Orange Blossom	Platinum
Yellow	Rosemary	Sunflower	Diamond	Saffron	Gold
Violet	Winter Savory	Lilac	Aquamarine	Lemon	Pewter
Blue	Balm	Narcissus	Sapphire	Nutmeg	Tin
Green	Alkanet	Rose	Emerald	Myrtle	Copper
Red	Anemone	Geranium	Ruby	Tobacco	Bronze

Table 10.3
Items for Your Balancing Medicine Bag

When you heal your psyche 'I', your somatic half 'Me' is also automatically healed of many diseases. Do not, however, overlook the help an RD – a regular doctor – can give you. Certainly not all diseases are altogether psychic; some diseases such as malnutrition, and heart strain induced by over-exertion, obviously are mainly somatic. There is therefore a whole list of diseases that should be regarded as the purview of the RD. It is true that you must repair the damage to the psyche caused by those somatic diseases; but do not assume that you can totally cure every disease just by doing a psychic healing. We always instruct our students most carefully that both they and their seekers[2] should first go to an RD when healing is needed. When he gives up the case or has little effect on it, then it is time to attempt a psychic healing; for when the RD cannot help, then in most cases it is the psyche that needs attention.

When your aid is requested in a healing case, your astral abilities will be more effective in healing the psyche than the somatic. One thing you should always look out for is the perpetual psychic hypochondriac. These people are always sick. They need a disease so that they will gain attention from those around them. They are basically incurable unless you change their lifestyle so they can learn alternative ways to gain attention without their manipulative diseases.

Observing Others on the Astral

There are two levels of observation you can undertake when you are out on the astral. First, you can view the mundane world, looking at the circumstances surrounding your seeker. Second, you can observe the astral entities, both of the seeker and of those people who are key players in his life and future. Taking each of these in turn:

Mundane-world observation – This is the easiest part of your healing and helping effort. All you have to do is to go to the location where your seeker says the problem is occurring. This could be his dwelling, the dwelling of an acquaintance, the office, or wherever the important action is. If you are an astral projector of the type that has to travel along a map to a location, these visits can become tiresome. You should instead learn as soon as possible how to go directly to the location of interest. To do this, you need what are called 'psychic links' to the person or the location. Table 10.4 shows

[2]In this context 'seeker' means the person who is asking you for help.

typical psychic links.

Special cases of psychic links are as numerous as grains of sand on the beach. Anything you can think of will work so long as it summons the scene or the person clearly to your

Links to a Person	*Links to a Place*
A recent photograph	A recent photograph
A sample of handwriting	Paint from a room wall or a thread from a carpet
Personal garment or trinket	Stick, stone, soil or wood from place
Nail clipping or hair	Hand-drawn map

Table 10.4
Psychic Links to People and Places

mind. One special case we are often asked about is a link to a car. Obviously a photograph will work. A tiny snipping from the upholstery, especially from the driver's seat, will work too; one thing that will not work in the case of a car is mud from under the mudguard. This psychic link will take you instead to the location where the mud was picked up. Apply your mind; if you think a certain item will work, it probably will. It is best, of course, to have more than one link; for then if one fails, you can use the other.

You should obtain the necessary psychic links from the seeker and, when you lie down to astrally project, have the links with you together with a definition of the problems you are attempting to solve. If your seeker makes excuses that amount to a refusal to provide the necessary psychic links for your work, then drop the case. He is in effect saying, 'I like my problem. I want to keep it so I can continue to complain to everyone around me.'

It is most important to keep in mind at all times during your effort that the seeker needs you more than you need him. In many cases you are wise to refuse aid until the seeker agrees to the conditions you set. Once you get into this type of guidance, you will have an abundance of seekers knocking at your door. It is completely impossible for you to help all of them, so take the ones who are most in need and who will co-operate with you. Dump the others, especially those who are not seriously ill, the minute you realize they are making you another victim of their sick little games.

When you project, go to the most appropriate location where you expect to find the solution to the problem. That is, observe the seeker in his interactions with his associates and intimates, and then observe the associates and intimates when the seeker is not present. In this way you can gain important knowledge about their attitudes towards him. Hundreds of simple questions can be answered in this manner: Is he going to get the pay-rise? Does she really like him? Is the boss telling the truth? Will there be a reconciliation? Who is manipulating whom? Et cetera, et cetera.

In making these observations, you may often wish to read documents. You do have the ability to lift and turn a few pages of a file, but you will find this is very tiring. Another approach is to will yourself down into a file and read the pages without turning them. This technique is faster and far less tiring than attempting physically to turn the pages.

Occasionally you will want to make it known that you are observing a scene, for instance, when someone doubts your ability. If someone is expecting you to be present and thus is in a receptive frame of mind, you can make your presence felt to him by doing such things as gently trying to pinch him or pulling a single hair or whisker. Contrary to popular belief, many cats and dogs show no reaction to the presence of an astral entity. We have no idea whether this is because certain animals have had the ability to see astral entities bred out, they can't see human astrals, or whether they are merely bored with something they see and feel all the time.

Astral-Entity Observation – If you see auras in your daily life in the mundane world, you may be surprised and disappointed when the 'I' and the 'Me' of the observed person are integrated. That is to say, your normal aura-seeing ability is limited to the observance of the auras of other astral entities, 'I's' separated from their 'Me's'. Once the 'I' is separated, however, seeing, feeling, hearing, sensing their innermost thoughts becomes extremely simple, a skill everyone can manage.

Historically, two solutions to this problem have been used: first, waiting until the 'I' of the person of interest separates naturally; or second, acting as a Guide while the other person is sleeping, and helping his 'I' to separate. The second of these solutions is obviously the more practical, though it means that you will have to astral project late at night, when you can reasonably expect the person of interest will be sleeping. Acting as a Guide is a multifaceted undertaking. You can be of tremendous help to other people in helping them realize the truths of the universe. You can also play malicious tricks on them, showing them fantasies derived from your own imagination that will scare them and prevent them from gaining the truth. The technique is the same in both cases; your intent is what makes the results good or evil.

In acting as a Guide, you must appear to the sleeping person's 'I' in an acceptable form. In the case of Christians, this is usually the guise of a wise, white-bearded Santa Claus sort of personality called Jehovah. It does not matter that this is not Jehovah's true guise as he is described in the Bible; for in the minds of most Christians, he is not an angry god, but is a benevolent sage. In the case of Pagans, the best guise to help a male seeker seems to be that of Isis or Diana, clad in revealing garb. In the case of Isis, the breasts are usually bare; and in Diana, a lot of leg is shown. To help a female seeker, you might choose to appear as the Horned God Cernunnos or as Pan or Priapus; in any event, in the guise of an attractive semi-clad male.

Persuading the 'I' to separate from the 'Me' is usually very easy. Some subjects have reported stubborn cases in which the 'I' refuses to leave, but this usually happens because your Guide-guise is inappropriate for the person you are working on. Come back the following night in a more appropriate guise, and in most cases the 'I' will happily be led into the astral realms.

When the 'I' is separated from the 'Me', you can immediately sense its true nature. 'I' is usually a fairly amenable character, very receptive to new ideas; thus you can usually persuade 'I' to look into your reflective pool and see its own problems. The 'I' will then quite often ask for help in solving them. If the problem will be solved by readjusting the 'I' you are working with, then that is the course you should take. We have never found any situation in which it is proper to withhold help from an 'I' that is maladjusted. As one human creature to another, it is only ethical to enlarge the understanding of that 'I' in every way you can.

Special-Case Observations

A special warning is in order when it comes to seekers who claim to be possessed, hexed, jinxed, under psychic attack, or in any way influenced by astral energies. Often when you travel out and watch them, you can see nothing. There is no evidence of any of the negative influences the seeker claims are operative in his life. The problem here is that none of these situations (with the possible exception of possession) is a continuous state. That is to say, you may not be around when the person is actually being influenced, so you get the impression that he is deluded. He may not be. It's just that you were not there at the time it happened.

The best way to deal with these situations is to get the seeker to prepare all the things needed for a protective circle around his room or his bed. Travel on the astral; make sure there are no unusual or suspicious energies attached to him or to his 'I'; then rapidly return to your body and either go to him and complete a protective procedure, or phone him and have him do it himself. This is a sure method of determining just how valid his complaint is because the seeker's life circumstances either will change, or they will not. If his circumstances change, then he was indeed under some form of attack. In this case, you must spend a lot of time waiting around on the astral to see precisely what this attack is.

If the circumstances do not change, then the seeker is merely playing games, blaming all his problems on the occult. This is a very easy and common thing for people to do. It is so convenient to have something to blame, something they think cannot be checked on or documented.

Diagnosis

When a seeker first comes to you he places his own personal interpretation and bias on everything he tells you. You will often be astounded as you astrally examine the situation, to find how badly distorted is his view of what is really going on. Typically, someone being passed over for promotion or a pay-rise never thinks he is not worth it. It's always the boss's bias that is holding him back. Well, in most cases it simply isn't!

The first part of your diagnosis, then, is to get the facts straight. Find out from your astral examination of the situation what is really going on and what is the motivation of the various players in this human drama. Write it down; many a seeker has developed great skill at persuading others that their observations are in error and that he is being totally misunderstood and abused.

The second part of your diagnosis must be an honest evaluation of the situation. From this evaluation you can lay out a plan of action that will lead to help for your seeker. The plan of action may, of course, be just a matter of getting him to realize that he needs to improve his own appearance and that the people around him are not part of some huge conspiracy against him. In cases of sickness, the most important fact you can establish is *why* the seeker *needs* the illness that he has.

Counselling

In discussing your tentative diagnosis and evaluation with the seeker, you must be most careful to be impartial. You are going to make him follow your instructions by influencing his 'I' while you are on the astral. You do not have to direct him to certain actions or accuse him of any shortcomings in his own personality or behaviour. He doesn't want to hear how changes in his own attitudes and habits will cure a situation. This type of confrontation we often call the 'yes, but' situation. Every time you suggest something to the seeker, he replies with a sentence that begins, 'Yes, but I can't do that because...' or 'Yes, but I'm certain it will never work because...' This leads only to your frustration and his anger. Nothing is accomplished. In his eyes you immediately become part of the conspiracy. The discussions you hold with the seeker should thus be limited to exploring possibilities in a detached, third-party kind of way. That is to say, you quote fictitious examples of people who have solved problems similar to his by following a certain course of action.

From these non-threatening third-party discussions, you can judge whether or not the 'Me' of the seeker thinks the solution is reasonable. Once you have 'Me's' concurrence that the proposed solution in the third party's case was reasonable, then you can confidently expect to influence the seeker's 'I' into getting his 'Me' to follow your guidance. During the discussion you may, of course, find flaws in your plan of action. Try to amend the plan so that these are eliminated. Once the seeker's 'Me' has concurred, you should take the next opportunity to guide the seeker's 'I' along the agreed path. Now the problem is out of your responsibility, and the seeker must choose to accept or reject the guidance.

In the case where the seeker fully accepts the occult, you can counsel with the aid of a crystal ball, the tarot cards, or any other occult method that you are familiar with. Hopefully, when you counsel in this manner, the counselling will guide the seeker along a path similar to the one your diagnosis has indicated. Do not, however, be surprised if the reading gives a slightly different result; that is, after all, what readings are all about. We caution that you should not use an occult method with anyone having the slightest resistance to its use; for he will set up mental blocks against the successful outcome of any path thus indicated.

Action

There are so many actions you might take that it is impossible to outline them all within the limitations of this book. However, some general categories of action have worked well in most healing and helpful situations.

a) Drop the case. This option is always available to you. You should not drop a case just because it is very complex, but rather drop it when the seeker's 'I' and 'Me' both refuse guidance.

b) Influence the seeker's 'I'. In this case you should act as a Guide as we instructed earlier in this book, first showing the 'I' its problems and then commanding it to shape up. This may not be sufficient; and, just as you did in your own life, you may have to bring tuned energies into the seeker's life to effect a permanent cure for the 'I's' problems. Pages 182-184 contain the information you need to do a ritual.

c) Influence the seeker by controlling his dreams. Dreams are the result of the 'I' communicating knowledge to the 'Me'. The best way to control a person's dreams is to arrange for the 'I' to leave and then telepathically send a dream to the 'Me'. For instance: in your Guide-guise you tell the 'I' to go on a specific observing mission. Then you place one of your astral hands on the back of the dispossessed 'Me's' neck and the other on its forehead. Visualize the scenes you want to send to the 'Me'. Nightmarish, memorable scenes are easiest. These should show the results that the seeker will experience if he continues to follow his present path. Follow the nightmarish dream with a pleasant, warm alternative dream showing the results of following the new path that you have discussed with him. Do not try to influence the seeker along a path that you have not discussed with him, for this results in confusion and can result in a psychosomatic disease if the 'Me' rejects the guidance.

d) Directly influence the seeker by ritual means. What this method really entails is the sending of your energies, tuned in the appropriate manner, to the seeker. There are thousands of different rituals you can use to accomplish this goal.

e) Possession and Attached Entities. Cases of possession and cases where a lower entity is attached to a person do occur. They are the easiest type of problem to deal with from the astral. First, in your Guide-guise, send the true 'I' off on a mission. Then assume some terrible Guide-guise aspect, and threaten the possessing or attached entity with painful and dire results if it does not promptly leave. The more terrible and the more imaginative your threats, the more quickly will the possessing entity leave. Of course it is true that you must think carefully about the Guide-guise that you assume for this work. It must be something or someone that is meaningful to the unauthorized presence.

A Typical Ritual for Helping or Healing

Rituals are simply the formal structure which allow you to be sure that all steps necessary to accomplish your aim are completed. Unfortunately the word 'ritual' has come to have negative or even sinister connotations. However, when we use the word, all we mean is a framework within which you can work.

STEP 1 Decide what type of energies are needed to accomplish your goal. From Table 10.2, determine which items will give you, the occultist, the energies you are then going to send on. Obtain as many of these items as you can.

STEP 2 Obtain a psychic link to the person to be influenced. (This may be the seeker, or another person who is unduly influencing the seeker.) Refer to Table 10.3 for the most appropriate psychic links.

STEP 3 Obtain the following equipment:

Parchment-type paper	Scent[3]
Quill pen	Uniodized salt
Candle[3]	Ink[3]
Length of fabric[3]	All-wood table

STEP 4 Choose a time and a place. You wish to select a time when you are reasonably sure that the subject of the ritual is asleep and psychically receptive. You will need a secure place where you will be undisturbed.

[3]Choose the appropriate scent or colour from Table 10.3.

We do not recommend that you use the room from which you normally astrally project, because rituals leave behind them feelings of emotional intensity, and these are very difficult to clean from an area. Thus, if you do a ritual in your astral-travel area, you may foul up future astral travels.

STEP 5 Get on with it! Place your table so that you can stand behind it and face in the general direction of the subject. Cover the table with the fabric; place on it your candle, your psychic links, and your energy keys. Using the quill pen and the ink, write on the parchment-type paper the intent of your ritual. Make it as short a phrase as is possible. Imagine you are sending a very expensive telegram. Surround every-thing on your table with a single large circle of salt. Touch each object with scent. Light the candle. Think about the seeker's problem and why this ritual will solve it. Visualize the results of the ritual as clearly as you can. Hold between your hands the parchment-type paper with the intent written on it.

Start to chant in a soft voice, 'Ee-aye-ee-aye-oh.' Repeat this chant in a gradually louder and louder voice until you are shouting it out at the top of your lungs. As you shout it out the last time, light the paper and let it burn. When it has burned out, clap out the candle with your hands and shout:

> Harmful influence, be gone!
> N——[4], take these energies!
> Power, Power, go from me!
> As I will, so mote it be!

Collect the ashes from the burned parchment-type paper, and place them in an envelope. They should either

[4]'N——' is the name of the target of the ritual.

be included in the medicine bag the seeker is wearing or, if the seeker resists the occult, they should be hidden in the seeker's bedroom.

Follow-up

In occult work it is extremely frustrating when you spend hours of time and effort with people – and then they simply don't bother to tell you how it all ended. One thing is certain though: if nothing happened, you'll hear from them! Silence in occult work is a sure sign of success. But you want and need more than this. You want feedback from them so you can tell whether or not you are being successful in your work. Although it sometimes is discouraging and frustrating, still you must contact the seeker for whom you have been working and find out what happened. Then try to judge whether the change that has come into the seeker's life is the direct or indirect result of your work. Consider carefully every change that comes into the seeker's life; for it is very likely that you caused them. Write down what you have learned, together with your written notes on your astral trips on the case and notes on counselling sessions and any ritual you may have performed. Later, when time has put everything into perspective, come back and read your notes. In doing this, you will gain confidence in your effectiveness, and new knowledge as to the true workings of our joint reality.

Summary

In this chapter we discussed one of the most rewarding aspects of astral projection: the healing and helping of others. Nothing can be quite as fulfilling as the sudden improvement in a loved one's condition that you can see was the direct result of your astral work.

CHAPTER 11
The Selfish Use of Astral Travel

The obvious question now is: Can I use astral travel for my own gain? The answer is: Yes.

It is impossible to live without affecting the future. You eat, you excrete, you walk around killing some bugs and breeding others. Who is to say whether an act will significantly change history? One mosquito slapped into oblivion may prevent a future epidemic and change the course of the nation. So since you are in the world and since you are going to affect its inhabitants anyway, why not do it deliberately and within an ethical system rather than passively drifting along without purpose, just living for something to happen from one meal or one orgasm to the next? In order to survive you must make a thousand little decisions daily, so why not make those decisions systematically to gain your ends? Or do you like living like a stone?

Table 11.1 contains some thoughts on your level of existence. Where are you in that table? We hope you are in the levels past 5, still actively seeking and trying new paths, defining your own reality. We hope too that you have not rigidified your world so much that when a Carlos Castaneda comes along your beliefs come crashing down around your head and you wind up in a mental home.

What you do is your choice. Within yourself you have many untapped powers. Even the Bible says it's so. Here is how St Paul put it:

In each of us the spirit is manifested in one particular way, for some useful purpose. One man, through the spirit, has the gift of wise speech; while another, by the power of the same spirit, can put the deepest knowledge into words. Another, by the same spirit, is granted faith; another, by the one spirit, gifts of healing, and another miraculous powers; another has the gift of prophecy, and another ability to distinguish true spirits from false; yet another has the gift of ecstatic utterance of different kinds, and another the ability to interpret it.

Jesus clearly stated,

Greater things than these shall you do.

Hosea's exhortation is one we should all pay heed to:

An if ye reject learning, I will reject ye.

Level	Name	Characteristic Thought Pattern
0	Stone	I am everything.
1	Resistance	I don't want to understand.
2	Indifference	I don't have to understand.
3	Hopelessness	I am a puppet in 'their' hands.
4	Interest	Maybe I could understand.
5	Self-satisfaction	I understand everything.
6	Seeker	I wonder whether that's right.
7	Awareness	I understand that I can't understand everything.

Table 11.1
Levels of Existence and Awareness

Good versus Evil for You

Healing is a wonderful gift, though the germs we destroy probably don't much like it. Because of our set of ethics we do continue to heal, believing that the higher creatures have more need to continue in their incarnation than do bacteria or viruses. This dichotomy requires us to have some very structured ideas about such things as good and evil.

Brine shrimps are most useful research animals. When they are fit and well, they are constantly copulating, so the voyeuristic researcher can tell the condition of his laboratory subjects at a glance. The shrimps can also be eaten. One researcher wired up some plants to a lie detector. He found that when he killed a shrimp in the next room, the plants reacted. Did the shrimp die in a good cause (especially since it was later eaten)? Do the hundreds and thousands of other laboratory captives, whatever their level of development, that die each year constitute a huge 'evil', or is that a 'good'?

People who are ill or starving or otherwise preoccupied cannot concentrate on new thoughts. Many religious systems have promised an easy life in the Hereafter – provided you suffer today's misfortunes with a smile and a stiff upper lip. Astral travel indicates the opposite is best. Use the powers you have developed to improve your present life. Then you can more easily move on into the abstract thoughts that will give you an ethical system to use in future 'good' work. If you are worried about ethics today and are stuck in the cesspit, and if you have to infringe someone's rights to get out, think of it as educational to the other person; it will help him develop. Don't make this putative infringement of rights an excuse to go on doing nothing and drowning in the shit of the world.

The 'Flashy Car' Simile

The Rig Veda describes the interaction between the spirit 'I' and the body 'Me' as like that between a driver and a chariot. A modern simile for this interaction would be the relationship between you and your large, new, flashy, petrol-guzzling car.

This car you bought has several unusual characteristics: it seems to have a built-in desire to self-destruct; it guzzles extravagant amounts of petrol; it blows gaskets; it races around trying to keep up with other cars; and given half a chance, it runs into the car in front. Not only that, but while doing all these antics it insists that you shall drive it. And it constantly disobeys your relatively weak commands.

Occasionally, it is true, you can switch the engine off and leave it; but even then it pulls and tugs at you because it keeps telling you that it needs more and more attention. Just as the body tells the spirit, 'I am hungry,' 'I am cold', 'I am too hot,' 'I need sex,' 'Keep me happy,' so your flashy car is the uncontrolled beast that you must learn to control lest in its self-destructive urges it drag you down with it. You, the spirit 'I', must learn to control the urges of your mundane body, 'Me'. If the urges are reasonable they should be satisfied or even satiated. Then when the body is at rest, you can get out and go travelling. This is the constant, endless battle that goes on within your own body: the battle between 'I' and 'Me', 'I' striving to control, 'Me' nagging for fulfilment. So the question is: how many of the beast's urges ideally should you control, and how many should you indulge? If the spirit inhabits the body in order to learn through it, is it not also true that the spirit should allow the body to fulfil as many of its desires as possible, as the other half of learning?

The spirit needs the body to learn from, just as you need some form of car if you are going to learn to drive. It is unrealistic to allow your car to self-destruct or to destroy other cars; but short of that, why should you not enjoy free and extended travel?

You can elect to drive a much more modest machine and, in doing so, you will save money and (perhaps more importantly) conserve a diminishing world resource. The demands of the more modest machine would be far less costly in time and effort than the large flashy car; but it won't attract any envious glances from other drivers.

Whatever car you drive it is sensible to maintain it in good condition. In order to enjoy your body for as long as possible and to get the quintessence of experience from it, you should maintain it in reasonable condition, not mistreating it as a hermit would, nor yet as a glutton does, and perhaps even keeping it trim enough to chase the occasional sleek foreign model.

Getting in Touch with Yourself

'Me' is out living it up, and 'I' has to go with it. All right: who is running whom? Does the car run the driver? Even the car, if it had a consciousness, would know that the driver eventually must sleep and must have experiences without it being present. Too many people in this modern world would allow their cars to run them. Advertising in all its various subtle ways helps 'Me' in this endeavour. It creates in 'Me' continuous needs and dissatisfaction with the status quo. This engenders a way of life in which you live from moment to moment or for the moment – a confused, unplanned situation. No plan you make can last, for by insisting on new toys 'Me' creates one crisis after another. If you are to get out of this control of 'I' by 'Me' you must get in touch with yourself. Communication must be established between 'I' and 'Me', and a ranking of priorities defined.

How much power does 'I' have to govern 'Me'? It has the ultimate power. When 'I' leaves permanently, 'Me' dies! In most people's lives it seems as if any control by 'I' is totally lacking. Through astral travel and through your dreams, you can find out at least some of what 'I' wants; and by using your astral-travel capability you can more easily fulfil 'Me's' demands, thus making 'Me' realize how important 'I' is to its welfare.

Being Your Own Lie Detector

Travelling in here-now brings the whole world within reach of your house. Most people have varying degrees of paranoia:

Does he or she really like me? Did he really mean that? What does the boss think of me? A thousand other questions come to mind. Yet only a few talented psychics can tell when an astral being is present in a room. This means you can spy on other people and never, never be detected. You can find out what they think about you. You can find answers to all those nagging little questions and put your mind at ease. You have the knowledge, you have the ability, to travel where you wish. All you have to do is overcome any ethical block you may have to doing it. Two old sayings that contradict one another come to mind:

> Eavesdroppers never hear good of themselves.
> Forewarned is forearmed.

Which of these is the more important to you is for you yourself to decide, a decision which must be made by both 'I' and 'Me'.

Using Your Astral Influence

One of the very practical and useful things you can do when you learn to astral travel is to influence decisions to be made by other people. When someone is due to make a decision that will affect your future, recommend strongly to him that he sleep on it. This will give you time to visit his astral self and attempt to influence that all-important decision before it is made. If you know that in the near future you will be interviewed for a job by Mr Big, visit him on the astral plane before the interview; then when you meet in the interview, Mr Big will have an immediate affinity for you. He will get that feeling of, 'I have met this person before. He is an old friend; I know him!' The getting-to-know-you stage of the interview can then be accomplished rapidly and smoothly, putting both of you at ease more quickly, and matters will proceed to a positive conclusion.

Influencing others through their dreams and on the astral is a proven technique. If your reality construct admits to such action, you can influence Mr Big positively towards yourself and negatively towards your rival. One way this has been successfully accomplished is to use the shape-changing aspects of the realms to appear to Mr Big in the guise of your competitor and do something unpleasant to him. Then you can positively influence Mr Big – perhaps even 'save his life' – on the astral in your own guise, in this way giving him a very favourable impression of your capabilities while degrading those of your rival.

Remember: in the higher realms you can be anything and you can do anything. Your own thoughts result in changes of shape, attire and place. These changes happen rapidly, and you should practise them before you try them as a method of influencing others; for sometimes you can become confused, and start feeling sick and giddy. It's as if you had just come off a roller coaster; the rapid changes of direction have made you queasy.

The Argument for and against Possession

Horror films have made the whole subject of possession one of instinctive repulsion. Possession is simply the inhabiting of a 'Me' by an unauthorized 'I'. In most cases it does no harm. You can let a friend drive your car, can't you? Sometimes indeed possession can be a very positive force. For instance if some hard-drinking, pill-popping, profane, whoring, unwashed bum is dragged to a charismatic church and 'receives the holy ghost', what has really happened? His body is possessed by the spirit of some dead person, a person more conventional than him. No wonder he immediately becomes super-virtuous, gasping to all and sundry how Jesus got him just in time. His real self has died – been evicted – and has been replaced by another spirit who (correctly or incorrectly) believes he can do a better job of living his life than he was doing.

Young married couples often wish to experience the actual feeling of their partners. By possessing each other's bodies even for brief moments, couples can understand one another so that questions as to the why and wherefore of the other partner's feelings never need to be asked aloud and each can better understand the other's motivations and true feelings. This should not be attempted if either partner has hidden reservations about their mate, for reservations that were previously deeply hidden will become crystal-clear to the possessing entity.

It is your own reality that establishes which of these cases are positive and which negative.

Possessions that make up the grist of lurid media presentation are those in which a negative entity possesses a young sweet thing and refuses to yield the body to its true spirit. We have yet to see any cases of claimed possessions of criminals and old or ugly people.

Using Possession to Your Advantage

With your present knowledge you can travel out and possess another body for any length of time you wish. Suppose there is someone whom you wish to influence, or whom you wish to become better acquainted with. Travel astrally to where he is asleep and watch him. You will see his astral self depart from the body on its own affairs. He has in effect left his body double-parked and idling as he might leave his car double-parked and idling as he pops into a shop to get some cigarettes. This is your chance. Slip into that idling body and run it around for a little while. How does it feel to be that most dread of all spirits, a 'possessing entity'?

Not only can you run his body around – drive his car – but you can now avail yourself of a matchless opportunity to learn how he thinks and what makes him tick. When you have learned what you need to know through being in his body, lay the body carefully down again – park the borrowed car without damaging it – and go and get into your own car.

Two things will immediately be apparent to you. One is the importance of psychic safeguards around your own body. You can now understand the importance of such things as circles and affirmations. Second is the fact that some choices are open to the possessor. Having once got behind the wheel of that borrowed car, you may either choose to give the car back to its rightful owner, or you may not. Because you have your own proper living body to return to, you will doubtless yield the possessed body to its rightful inhabitant.

You will find with practice that you can not only understand the person you possessed far better than before, but you can also make him or her understand your point of view more clearly. Some tests have shown that you can go back through time and converse with people long-dead. There are hints that you can travel back and actually possess the body of someone who lived in the past. Such an action would give you an intimate knowledge of the thought processes of, for instance, Napoleon or Churchill. The Institute has far too few factual data on this aspect of possession to say whether or not it really works as well as we believe it can.

The Law of Attraction – 'Like Attracts Like'

It is said in occult circles that a man called Hermes Trismegistus (thrice-greatest) wrote the original Law of Attraction on an emerald tablet and gave it to an Egyptian priest so it would be for ever enshrined in the world's thought. A modern catchphrase for the Law of Attraction is:

'Birds of a feather flock together.'

Not only do people of the same disposition and interests eat together in the works canteen; it is also true that when you have an unpleasant disposition, unpleasantness will surround you. When you expect disaster, it happens. In his famous book[1] Norman Vincent Peale showed how thinking positive gave positive results. This special application of the Law of Attraction works irresistibly to help you in the modern world.

When you set out to influence others to your way of thinking and thereby gain your ends, you might ask, 'What effect will this enterprise have on my spiritual development? Will a backlash inevitably occur and make me sorry?' In general our research has shown that no such backlash occurs. The occasional cases that we have found where disaster followed attempts to influence the outcome of events have led us to these rules that you can use to guide you:

1. *Motivation* – Ask yourself what is truly motivating your action. Is it to gain comfort? To acquire sufficient money so that you won't starve? Or is it something way beyond that? Something that 'Me' wants but doesn't really need? If you can honestly say the result of your action will allow you to spend more time astral travelling, yet will not cause pain or humiliation to another human being, you can generally proceed without fear.

2. *Retaliation* – We are all human. When you've been 'done' it is a very natural response to wish for retribution. It is best if you arrange this in such a manner as to teach rather than just punish.

3. *Money* – Yes, get a better job. Yes, see if you can find out which horse will win. We strongly believe that you cannot adequately explore the spiritual realms while you are living on the edge of poverty. Money is not evil; sometimes the actions of people in gaining money are evil by conventional standards, but money is merely a coin of

[1] *Power of Positive Thinking.*

exchange. It has no moral colour of its own.

4. *Harm to others* – Provided you do not infringe on another entity's rights, you should play the game of life to the fullest. If another entity loses the race that you are running with it, then it learns that it will have to run a better race next time. This does not mean that you are evil for having won. The question you should ask yourself is: When you win, will you be happy with yourself?

The Future Depends on the Past

This truism gains more meaning when you have learned from your astral-travel experiences that the past is immutable whereas the future is still mutable. Many inexperienced experimenters believe they can find themselves in the future, think themselves a new lifestyle in that realm, and it will magically come true. THE FUTURE IS FOR EVER MUTABLE. Thus as soon as you turn your back on your new magic future and come back and resume your old slothful lifestyle, the magic future disappears and re-forms itself the way it was before. The only way to make permanent changes in the future is to have a life plan that will lead to that magical lifestyle you desire. As Socrates said so long ago, the unexamined life is not worth living. Take a moment and examine your life. Astral travel is not a free ticket to a lifetime of laziness.

It is not too late. You can sit down today and decide what you want and how to get there. Of course each person is different, and your goals may not be the same goals as those of your next-door neighbour. High on most people's list of goals is the acquisition of money. We personally are more interested in increasing the general awareness of the people we meet than in the gaining of wealth.

Selecting Your First Step

Fortunately, astral travel can help you in your allocation of priorities. By travelling in the nearest future realm, you can see what you will lack in the future if you continue on the path you are now following. Examine the list in Table 11.2. Either make your own list and shuffle your wishes around until you are satisfied, or simply mark on this page with a pencil which is your first priority. For this priority to become a reality you need a plan of action.

Money	A Better Job
Serenity	Improved Health
Friendship	A New Lover
Psychic Awareness	

Table 11.2
Priority Assessment

A word of warning if you are using astral techniques to capture and hold a new mate. So far in this book you have learned many techniques for finding friendship and influencing others. You should be aware that when you use a controlling technique for such a purpose you will never know afterwards whether the mate stays because of love or because of astral control.

An Imaginary Example

Josephine is a fictitious person, just as Liz and Bert were. However, the things she does in this example are all authenticated by letters in the Institute's files.

Josephine became a widow with one small child when Derek, her junior executive husband, died of a heart attack. Her serene life in a fashionable flat in London was shattered. She had no friends of her own. The social life that she and

Derek had shared had always been company-orientated, but once the firm had paid her the small insurance benefits that came due on her husband's death, she no longer saw any of its members. Loneliness, sorrow, self-pity, all took their toll and to recover from the depression in which she found herself, she started taking 'uppers'. The next few months of her life drifted by in a haze, a haze she cannot describe. Pills followed pills in an endless succession, until inevitably she woke up in a hospital bed with her daughter a ward of the court.

One thing she did vividly remember from her drug experience was travelling without her body in other realms. These trips were so real to her that she was afraid she had somehow damaged her mind and was on the verge of madness. Eventually, with much trepidation, she told the sympathetic hospital psychiatrist of her fears. He was a man who had had many occult experiences. He shared some of his with her, and they compared her view of the astral with his, finding many things in common between them. Assured now that she was not mad, Josephine was released from hospital and told that as soon as she could establish a household she could have her daughter back. Josephine had no job skills. She borrowed a little money from her parents to live on, but it was sufficient for no more than a stopgap. In this situation she decided she would experiment with her new-found astral-travel capabilities. Without training, without very much knowledge at all, she travelled several nights into the astral with the aid of pills. On two trips she clearly saw an ad for a social director cum assistant manager for a seaside resort hotel in Tenby in South Wales. On the second trip, when she saw the ad in more detail, she was able to identify the newspaper in which it was placed. She found the ad in the mundane world and applied for the job. Because she was unsure of herself and her abilities, she travelled on the astral to the hotel and watched the manageress at work. From this observation she grew confident that she could sell herself into the position and could handle it well after she got it.

With the use of a very little astral influence, she got the job. She was able to re-establish herself in a modest manner, and recuperate both her physical well-being and her relationship with her daughter in the festive attitude of the seaside resort. In her search for answers to the questions she had about her trips without her body, she finally found the Canterbury Institute and became one of its researchers. She was over-joyed to learn that she did not have to use pills to trip out and gain the ecstatic state that she now felt she could not do without. Her systematic investigation of the realms under the tuition of the Institute's leadership allowed her to get her obsession with the astral under control. Once this was done, she was able to reassure her daughter on the astral that she really was well again and would never again crawl down the neck of a pill bottle.

Life in the hotel was happy; new friends and romantic interludes abounded. But she had that feeling that she was on a pleasure boat about to leave the dock. The impermanence of the situation finally began to weigh on her. She asked for guidance on the astral, and was told in no uncertain terms that she should remarry and move to a farm. Having received the guidance, she asked for direction to her new mate. This came as an astral vision of a funeral notice that had appeared some five years before. She tracked down the notice in an old Tenby newspaper and from it found the widower who was living in squalor in an old farmhouse on the downs. The boldness with which she had to approach him was alien to her, but he accepted and welcomed it. It was apparent the couple knew one another and they instantly grew close. Since they had never met on the physical level, they must have had prior relationships on the astral. We recently received a letter from Josie. Let's look at her own description of her new life:

From high-fashion London to Wellington boots on a farm. From plenty of money to almost none. All this because of my astral journeys. I've never been happier. Initially I found it very difficult to cope with the long hours, the mud, and the muck. But every hour I put in meant that I got physically better and that I could see the changes I was making in my own environment. Initially I wanted to get everything done today, as I would have in London. Finally the realization came that getting the physical surroundings fixed up was far less important than making sure that the animals were comfortable. The simple life is truly for me. The days when I took pills to block out my sensations are gone. Now I savour every odour, even if it's of the midden. Now I savour every bite I eat, for most of it came from our own farm. Bless you for helping me. We don't have much money, but here's a little donation to help with the work.

Start Your New Life Today

Josie used her astral-travel abilities to get what she wanted. By asking questions on the astral she found out how to proceed. By using the astral she helped herself achieve the goals she had defined with her astral guides. Yes, she took advantage of her astral knowledge to gain her ends, but we don't think she did anything negative or damaging to her spiritual self in using her astral knowledge to improve her life. In fact, we would encourage you to follow the example she set, though perhaps in a more systematic way.

1. Establish your most urgent need. Sit down for a moment and decide what single thing it is you need most. If this answer always comes back 'money', or a 'new car', or something of this nature, then ask for an answer on the astral instead of on the mundane conscious level. In most cases you will get an entirely different answer from 'I' than you did from 'Me'. 'I's' answer is the one you want. 'I' is in command.

2. Fulfil your need. In no case will you get guidance on the astral that cannot then be followed. It may seem difficult;

it may involve giving up things which you hold dear; but if you wish to have a serene, contented life like the one Josie made for herself, you must follow your guidance.

We are by no means recommending that everyone become farmers. We are very definitely saying that you should work at a task which fulfils your needs as a person. This task could be metalworking, ditch-digging, office work, or any of the millions of other tasks that make the world go forward. The one thing your guides will not let you do is drop out from the system and go on some form of welfare. For without work, without hardship, without the competition of the world, there will be no growth.

Summary

There is no great cosmic law that prevents you from using every little capability you have to get ahead and to fulfil yourself in life. The team that wins using new tactics is admired. The team that loses is scorned. In order to get ahead without damaging your spiritual development, you must still be able to live with yourself. As you progress, so you may grow to dislike some of the things you did to gain your position. This in itself is a very positive sign that you are developing on the spiritual levels. Many times the things we did yesterday are not the things we would do today.

Provided you learn from your mistakes
Provided you can leave them behind
You are surely progressing.

CHAPTER 12
Serenity through Astral Knowledge

In conventional reality the dog wags his tail. If the dog's tail became heavier than the dog, it would perhaps wag him. As western society has progressed along its materialistic track, so our tails have become increasingly heavy and more likely to wag us. The driver should be in control of the car – but too much of the time the car runs the driver's life. Getting a set of values which lends even equal weight to 'I' and 'Me' is beyond the ability of most people. Instead of developing their own standards by investigating the astral and the internal relationship between 'I' and 'Me', they are given arbitrary, inflexible rules of conduct from external sources and ever more demands are placed on them by the out-of-control 'Me'.

Anyone with an ounce of initiative will naturally kick against external rules and do everything in his power for a chance to taste the forbidden fruit. 'Thou shalt not,' no matter in what form it is said, cannot be a successful motivating factor; anyone with drive will resist it. The way to develop a realistic set of values and to get people to abide by them is to encourage everyone to experience the astral side of his own life. From these experiences people can gain understanding of life's underlying meaning and of the effect negative behaviour patterns have on their own progress. Such 'great experiments' as the American Prohibition graphically demonstrate this fact: inflicting unrealistic laws from the outside leads to 'evil' rather than 'good' behaviour. If someone handed you a box and said, 'Here are your new shoes. Wear them and like them or else,' it would not take you long to realize that he wasn't quite normal. However, when people understand the reasons for laws they tend to abide by them.

How to Start

In fairness to yourself, after having read this far and
hopefully having experienced some of the astral-travel
phenomena that so many others have shared, you should
now reassess your reality construct, assing to it those things
from the astral-travel phenomena that can be called 'general
facts', and (if you are so inclined) adding facts which can be
gained by the answers astral guides give you to your questions. Logic demands that this be done in sequential steps.
First, establish where you are today. Second, add the ideas
you really feel confident of. Then, third, extend this new
reality by adding to it the facts gained from your astral
guides.

What Do You Believe?

What are your real beliefs? No one is looking over your
shoulder. Sit down and make a few notes on the issues of
today, on such topics as ethics, politics and medicine. Read
some more books. You mean you've never done this before?
Is it perhaps that you have never thought about what you
really believe? Is it perhaps that you have taken at face value
a set of second-hand beliefs that were developed in medieval
times? Now is the time to get your attitudes and ideas sorted
out.

This is often so threatening that many people prefer to do
it while sitting on the lavatory behind a locked door. If you
do it there, you can be sure that if you don't like them or
don't want anyone else to see them — you can flush them
down the pan. Shouldn't you keep some of them? Aren't they
really worth more than the rest of the stuff you flush away?
Are you going back to those ancient and medieval ideas
'they' say are right and that you have taken as gospel? Or are
they now fit only to be flushed away?

Axioms from the Astral Travel Computer

Every person's perception of the general reality in which we all exist is slightly different, yet many parts of this general reality are amenable to statistical definition. We cannot say what the colour 'green' means to everyone. You were told at an early age, 'That is green,' but what does it look like? Just because both you and your neighbour call the spring grass in your lawn 'green' does not necessarily mean that you both perceive it in the same way; but we all call it green. In just the same way, in the spiritual and astral realms there seem to be general reality rules that are amenable to statistical analysis. Summarizing the most important of these axioms:

1. *The realms themselves* – It is quite clear that there are genuine areas of reality which you can experience by going through the process we call 'astral travel'. What this process actually is may be in doubt; but statistically there can be no doubt that a structured otherworld exists and that this otherworld can be experienced by people willing to train themselves to enter it. It is further clear that your physical body is left behind when your consciousness enters these realities.

2. *The guidance system* – A logical methodology is in force in the astral realms. Within its framework teachers from 'higher' levels of the system come 'down' to help those who need guidance. The guidance system seems to be used both to help those who are searching and to teach those from upper levels by having them teach. Learning by teaching is, of course, a well-known technique universally employed on the mundane.

3. *Graduation* – Moving up through the astral realms by discarnate spirits is a process of learning and graduation. The most significant lessons to be learned in these gradua-

tions seem to be the virtues of selflessness and the relinquishing of individual biases and desires.

4. *Melding* – A necessary part of the learning process is the
surrender of individuality in which three small spirits meld
into a larger entity and individuality and ego are
necessarily suppressed. The new entity combines the
learning of the three spirits that it contains but during the
melding process many cultural and sexual biases seem to
be eliminated.

5. *The space-time continuum* – Man's inquiring mind has
always been fascinated by the stars. In recent years our
understanding of those heavenly bodies has grown
immeasurably. Thus travelling in the cosmic realm has
become easier both to understand and to accomplish. The
converse is true of the time domain. With our scientific
outlook it is more difficult to comprehend that time is
merely part of a reality-construct and is not something
fixed which we experience for a moment and then lose for
ever.

6. *Consensus reality* – The higher you progress in the astral
realms, the more variability comes into the setting. In
many of the higher areas the setting is changed by your
least thought. As you come back down from these levels,
your thoughts can still make changes in the settings, but
only when such thoughts are firmly held and you have an
intense desire to make the change you want. You can feel
the acceptance or rejection of your thoughts by the group
surrounding you in a lower cultural level when you wish to
make a change in an area. Some researchers report that in
the guidance level of the here-now they can still make
changes in the setting, but that their ability ceases when
they enter the here-now realm. The lower levels are thus
the result of the group's thought patterns – a consensus
reality.

7. *Death and rebirth* — An extension of the work that the Canterbury Institute has been doing is the observation from the astral of births and deaths. Statistics are extremely fragmentary at present, but there are sufficient data to indicate that the guidance system of the astral extends back to the physical world. That is, spirits who are not ready to meld from the here-now guidance level have to return to inhabit another body and learn by this experience before they can progress.

Axioms from Astral Guides

The axioms in the previous paragraphs are taken from statistical analysis of reports of astral travels. A smaller group of researchers were programmed to ask specific questions of the astral guides. Their answers show more statistical deviation than is apparent from the analysis of actual observation. We suggest that you take each of the following axioms with the proverbial grain of salt until you too have gone into the astral and have asked the same questions. You will then be able to correlate the answers you receive directly with the following tentative axioms.

1. *Reincarnation* — As schoolchildren move up through classes, so the spirit graduates from a body into the astral and either progresses upwards or returns and inhabits another earth-plane shell to learn new lessons. An extension of this axiom is the idea of spirits being developed in less-complex beings, like animals, on their way into the human levels and that the entity that leaves the human level through the last human gateway is on its way to inhabit a more complex body, either in the inner space of this planet or on another planet. Some support for this concept is found in guides' answers to questions and from the fact that there are no animal spirits in the human astral realms.

2. *The Deity* – Nothing we have learned in all the astral work requires a deity. To explain the Source or the First Cause, a deity is a desirable convenience. Many of the guides believe in an Ultimate Deity, but whether this is because of earth-plane training or through actual knowledge is very much open to conjecture. The further up the system the question was asked, the less definite became the answer. Other reality constructs based on the interchange of time, matter and energy, seemed at these high levels to be of equal weight as the concept of an Ultimate Deity.

3. *Hell* – The axiom that hell does not exist will, we are sure, soon be listed under the observable axioms rather than finding itself here among the less provable concepts. There have been very few observations of a place of torment or a place of forced learning, so few as to be statistically meaningless. Occasionally guides are found who refer to hell, though none has visited it. The concept that hell is really the earth-plane to which you must return if you do not graduate from the here-now seems to be the most acceptable concept to the majority of guides.

4. *Thoughtforms* – In the lower astral realms amorphous clouds of energy in various shapes drift around. The guides say quite definitely that these are thoughtforms, either negative energies that have not found a target, or prayers to various deities. These thoughtforms do affect the realms. Sometimes they take on the shapes of strange monsters, and at other times they seem to lighten the area around themselves. In all cases they should be avoided, for they are real; that is, thoughts are real things.

A Possible Reality Construct?

Three years ago a special meeting of successful researchers was called by the Canterbury Institute. Some forty-eight people attended and spent a long, sometimes acrimonious, weekend in which they postulated a general reality construct. The following paragraphs are our own report on what they agreed to. We recognize that our report is biased by our own reality construct. Further, it should not for one moment be thought that all the ideas were held by all the researchers. The discussion was, as we have said, acrimonious. Discussions of spiritual matters where no holds are barred tend to be this way. Spiritual matters discussed within the framework of dogma are of course devoid of interest.

The hypothesis is for ever growing and developing. More – much more – unbiased research information is needed. That is the *raison d'être* for this book, and that is why we ask you so sincerely to complete the questionnaires after you have genuinely travelled through the realms.

Reincarnation

General agreement was reached on the idea of reincarnation as a learning process. The spirit, your 'I', is immortal. It never dies; it only grows. This 'I' is separable from your 'Me' or body. The way your 'I' controls your body determines your destiny. 'I' should control 'Me'. The spirit is reincarnated on this earthplane in this specific identity so that from controlling a body of this type it may learn what it is like, for instance, to undergo such experiences as pain, hunger, anger, love and disappointment.

When the body dies, the spirit casts it aside as a snake does its outgrown skin; the spirit then proceeds to the here-now astral level where it can either progress or return to take on another identity. An extension of this basic idea was generally agreed; it said in effect that spirits of lesser developed beings came from other developmental areas to inhabit human shells.

It was theorized that when a microbe dies, its spirit goes

into Side. If that elemental spirit is judged ready to progress, it is given a more complex earth-plane identity to work with. So as the spirit learns, it is given gradually more complex living organisms to inhabit. At each level the spirit must gain complete control of the organism entrusted to it before it progresses.

This idea is sometimes described as the 'boarding-school simile'. Figure 12.1 shows it as a progression. The spirit comes from its home in Side where it has absorbed the lessons it learned in its previous earth-plane incarnation, and on the earth-plane inhabits a body selected for its suitability. When it has learned all it can from this body in turn, the body dies and the spirit returns to Side. Eventually, after many incarnations, the spirit is ready to progress to higher planes. Thus it is up to you to make sure that while it is in a body the spirit undergoes as many experiences as you can arrange for it.

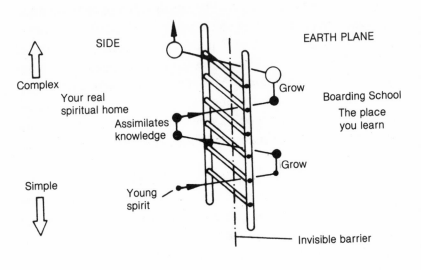

Figure 12.1
The Boarding-School Simile

There is no backslipping from a complex to a simpler being; that is, if you are 'bad' you won't 'transmigrate' or reincarnate as a lower-level animal. None of the researchers had any reports to give on any record of their progress held in any great book or akashic hall. The whole theory of the threat system called 'karmic debt' appears to be a myth invented by the Law-Giver Manu.

Suicide, which can be looked upon as an attempt to drop out from the system, seems to guarantee another incarnation at the same level. None of the researchers felt that the human level was necessarily the most complex or the last of the assignments on the physical plane. The ultimate aim of each spirit is to learn and grow and finally to rejoin the Source. All ignorance, negation and selfishness had to be washed out of the spirit before it could progress from the human level. Some researchers openly wondered whether these attributes were purely human, noting for instance that many animals exhibit selfless behaviour.

There was some discussion on what was 'alive' and what was 'dead'. Some felt that because of atomic motion even inanimate objects are in fact alive; others limited their definition of 'life' and hence their reincarnation thinking, to things like microbes and lichens which are at the very bottom rung of the accepted ladder of life.

The physicists among the researchers tended to look on spirits as tiny energy packages that started as minute charges and gradually grew more and more complex, carrying with them in complex computer-like codes their accomplishments. The melding of entities results in the threefold expansion of the energy being carried by the entity.

The Growth Theory

A very neat and workable hypothesis was formed as to the meaning of life and the reason that life is becoming ever more complex. Figure 12.2 is a simplistic representation of this hypothesis. A minute energy package comes down to the earthplane from the Source and inhabits a shell. Through the reincarnation process the energy package grows and expands. Eventually it rejoins the Source, thereby increasing the size of the Source. Since the Source is pure energy, the energy packages that rejoin it must also be pure energy; that is to say, they must be of the same high frequency as the Source, and cleansed of any negative energies.

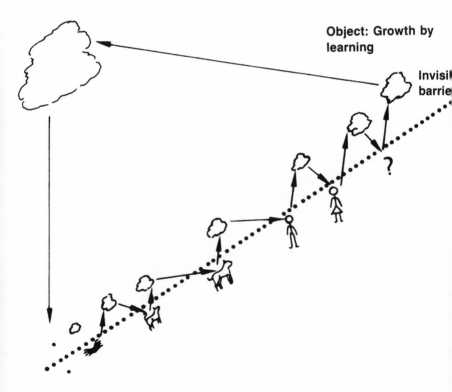

Figure 12.2
The Source as Energy

It was agreed that there is much confusion on the nature of the Source and on Its confusion with a deity. The Ultimate Deity is obviously beyond our human form and is so far beyond our understanding that It is indefinable. Even the Source, when we define It as 'an energy package' cannot be the Ultimate Deity; for by defining It we limit It; whereas by definition, the Ultimate Deity must be non-evidential. It can be realized only intuitively, not scientifically.

Prayer

The abundance of loose thoughtform packages in the lower levels of the astral caused much concern among the conferees. It was agreed that as a general principle they were the result of prayer or directed thoughtforms of other sorts. The conferees agreed that prayer was thus a negative influence and should be discouraged.

The positive approach to fixing one's life problems is to travel into the astral and make something happen. Railing against those people who hate one, and praying, are both counterproductive efforts. It is especially true that prayer should be avoided, if it indeed ruins the spiritual landscape.

Reality

Three realities were hypothesized.

1. *Personal* – This reality is constructed by your own spirit making its own visible throughtforms in areas that were previously empty. It comes fully into play when you visit the variable astral realms. The scene you see is totally under the control of your own thought patterns. It is personal to you. As soon as another entity enters the area, control of the scene is shared and it becomes a type 2 reality.

2. *Consensus* – This reality is the result of the interaction of two or more spirits on an empty space. A consensus reality is the product of the thoughtform packages produced by all present in any area. In this view the whole world is a consensus reality of all the thoughts of the spirits that are present in it. The astral realms themselves are a consensus reality.

3. *General* – This is actually the perception of a consensus reality by an individual entity. The reality seen is that reality that everybody sees. It is relatively fixed because it has been formed over aeons of time by millions upon millions of spirits, some of which are no longer present.

The general reality is often perceived in a distorted manner by individual entities. This is not a distortion of the reality by the entity, but instead results from internal biases on the part of the viewer. It is as if the viewer were wearing astigmatic or coloured glasses, not the result of a change in the consensus reality.

Your personality reality is totally in charge of the scenery in the variable astral realms. As you descend through levels towards the here-now, the effect of your personal reality on the consensus reality lessens. The strength of your personal convictions and will power determines the effect you can have on the consensus reality. People with PK (psychokinetic) ability have very strong intent and thus can bend the consensus reality to their will. It is to be noted that at the higher levels of the astral realms the reality becomes bland and devoid of scenery; this indicated to the researchers that those who have developed beyond the variable realms either have no control over, or feel no wish to control, their environment. Thus the demonstration of PK ability or other psychic parlour tricks has a negative correlation with spiritual development.

The Problem of Hell

Since millions of Christians for countless ages have believed in and thought about hell as the place for punishment and discipline, why can we not find it? It should be part of the consensus reality, but in fact it does not seem to exist. Conceivably the oddly shaped monster clouds of unused 'prayer' in the astral here-now could be thought of as devils; however, no personification of a being like the Hollywood version of Satan seems to exist. If Satan is indeed a part of our heritage, he should, damn it, be around.

Zonal Time

The consensus realities of other time zones are already in existence. Those from time past are immutable, while those from time future are still being formed by the forward-thinking entities of today. Many discussions were held on the reasons for the zonal effect in which only certain portions of these general realities were available for visit. No conclusion could be reached on this matter, and it was agreed that more research was needed into the precise time zones that a group of astral travellers can reach together. If it is found that the zones are common among many astral travellers, these zones would be part of a consensus reality construct built by a consensus which decided that entities should not be able to travel freely in the time domain. It can also be hypothesized that in the consensus time-space continuum only certain realities can intersect with one another at a given place and time.

Good and Evil

In the general opinion of the conference, evil could best be defined as the preventing of development in another spirit, and good could be defined as helping a spirit to grow and develop. When we apply this precept in our daily life, some interesting facts emerge.

Welfare prevents people from learning the hardships attached to real poverty and hunger. It thus prevents their spirit's development. Rules and regulations similarly discourage thinking and also prevent a spirit's development. When you give money or define a path to be followed, you encourage dependence in a host–parasite relationship. When you give gentle guidance, tools to do a job with, and learning experiences, you encourage autonomy and the development of the spirit.

Much discussion centred around the rights of a higher being when it came to cutting off the life of a lesser. Did this in fact constitute preventing the development of a spirit? And did it mean, for instance, that all cow spirits or potato spirits are for ever stuck in an endless cycle because none is allowed to die a natural death and complete its earth-plane development?

Many felt that the process of selecting the new body into which a spirit reincarnated could not be a random hit-or-miss process, and that spirits entering bodies that would be diseased, malformed or had a high probability of a short lifespan would know this before they reincarnated. It is reasonable to believe that many spirits must die many times in pain and terror before they have learned all there is to know about the horrors of such deaths. If the memory of such deaths was stronger in reincarnated humans, there would be less evil in the world. Apparently memories of past events are almost totally obliterated by the melding operation.

This concept neatly responds to current arguments for and against abortion, in that if the spirit knows it is going to be aborted, and still selects the body, it cannot be a sin to abort. Similarly, if a spirit knows that it will inhabit a body which is crippled, the artificial keeping alive of such a body might be considered an evil, for it delays the spirit's progress.

The Increasing Complexity of Life

Comparison of the past with the present clearly shows that the general reality is getting more complex. This is not just a feeling each generation has in turn, but is clearly an objective part of the general reality. Since the general reality is a consensus reality, and since science will continually discover more of the complexities of the world and technology will continually provide us with more complex machines, the general reality is bound to continue growing in complexity. Living in the more complex reality must necessarily be more difficult than was living in a simple reality construct. If the earthplane is indeed a school where spirits grow by learning, it is not surprising that the spirits are set ever more complex tasks; for in this manner the spirits learn more and grow larger. We can look forward to successive reincarnations, each into more complex realities, either on this plane or in some other locale.

The Ten Commandments

A minister at the conference presented us with a new view of these old chestnuts. He suggested we look at the ancient rules with our new dawning awareness and regard them as guidelines rather than commandments. We did and found that some interesting conclusions can be drawn. After overcoming the negative connotations of the word 'commandment' and softening the didactic and confining tone of the doctrine, we examined whether they are still applicable in our new reality.

'Thou shalt not commit adultery.'

What effect does the committing of adultery have on the

spirit's development? Is it negative or positive? In a permissive society where concealment of adultery is not required, there would be no negative effect; in fact the real husband might pay a little more attention to his wife. Further, the whole marriage and monogamy concept could well be discarded so that from the legal point of view adultery would cease to be possible. Why then this commandment?

Many spirits get stuck in the lower levels of the here-now in a constant round of sexual melding. This delays their development. Was this commandment, therefore, meant to apply on the astral and meant to be advice on how to progress more quickly?

'Thou shalt not steal.'

When 'I' gives in to 'me' and gets all the things that 'Me' demands, the learning-through-ordeal process is halted. This is especially true if trinkets and wealth are obtained without any effort. Thus stealing is a short-circuiting of the normal growth and development process.

'Thou shalt not bear false witness.'

On the astral, where telepathic communication takes over and the visible aura means that everyone's desires and emotions are visible, lying is not possible. In order to get a head start on your development, the avoidance of lying on the earthplane is desirable. 'Lying' in this sense is not taken to mean the avoidance of hurt by the telling of lies, but rather the gaining of a deceitful end. There is still in this life room for tact.

'Thou shalt not murder.'

Clearly killing someone prevents completion of their development cycle. Even if the victim be a murderer locked up for the most heinous crimes, still by cutting short the life, development is prevented.

'Thou shalt not covet . . .'

Coveting anything means a locking on to materialistic values, values that you must discard before you can progress up through the realms. Using the 'less is best' and 'small is beautiful' philosophies in your life will lead to more rapid development.

'Thou shalt not make graven images . . .'

Defining the Source or the Ultimate Deity is quite impossible. It is a useless, fruitless task. Therefore time spent in making any image, even a verbal image, of the Source is wasted. The limiting of the Source's power by defining it is palpably ridiculous.

'Thou shalt have no other god. . .'

The Source, no matter what It is, is the only source. It is; It always has been; It always will be. No matter what god or goddess you worship, it is not the Ultimate Deity but only a minor facet of It. However, all people have a need to worship something, so graven images of deity facets will probably always be idolized. It is very difficult to worship in terms 'I love you, you great indefinable something I don't understand.' It is quite noticeable in the commandments that Jehovah does not command the people to worship him; only that they do not worship graven images. This is the identical conclusion that the Canterbury Institute conference reached: i.e., that prayer should be discouraged because it messes up the lower astral levels with ill-defined thoughtforms.

'Honour thy father and thy mother.'

Throughout the centuries there has always been a generation gap between children and their parents. This means that children tend not to take guidance from elders. Quite apart from the mundane problems this engenders, if children will not take guidance on the earthplane, they will not learn to take it on the astral and thus will delay their own development.

Examining the commandments leads to the conclusion that if they are looked at from a mystical point of view they really aren't all that bad. It is only when they are used as a rod to drive and control people that they become negative.

Applied Awareness in Your Life

Through astral travel you gain not only mundane things to make 'Me' happier in this world, but also great spiritual understanding and serenity. Astral travel is not a religion; it will, however, form your belief system and help you define your path not only through this but also through future lives.

The priest, the minister, the shaman, the guru all work within their own rigid realities. Finding one of these spiritual 'leaders' equipped to interpret the astral for you is almost impossible. Many of them have never thought it necessary to explore on their own. They take the word of their own particular dogma and interpret it. This is a double interpretation; the wise avatar who originally travelled in the spiritual realms and reported to his followers on his experiences interpreted what he was seeing in the language of his time. Now, after many translations and modernizations, the word is reinterpreted again so that the laity can understand it in today's terms. The words assuredly have within them clues to the astral consensus reality; however, you know a far better way to find out the truth.

Go there yourself.
Go today. Don't delay.

If you wait around, whether it be for a new guide to take you by the hand, for that nice new blanket you're going to use, or for that new house that will have the space you need to work in, you might as well give up now. You will never smell the flowers. You will never experience the Ultimate.

In a world which is ever more complex and more difficult to live in because of the emphasis on the materialistic, the only way the consensus reality can be changed for the better is for more and more people to work at changing that reality. One person by himself or herself can change his own life and can change the world in a small circle around himself. For the future good of all, more people must understand the astral realms and what life is all about. You can play your individual part in this great drama of survival, or you can simply ignore it.

There is a place to start: that is where you are.
There is a time to start: that is now.
It exists. It is. Explore it.

APPENDIX A

QUESTIONNAIRES USED FOR STATISTICAL ANALYSIS

In addition to the following questionnaires, a comprehensive personal history was completed as part of the registration procedure.

AFTER YOUR FIRST TWILIGHT-ZONE ASTRAL TRAVEL

1. Answer the following questions 'true' or 'false'.

    a. When you are in the astral here-now,
       A car can pass through you. _____
       A man with an axe can harm you. _____
       A ferocious beast can harm you. _____
       Another astral entity can hit you. _____

    b. When you astral travel,
       Your personality changes. _____
       You become pure. _____
       Your personality does not change. _____
       The world is colourless. _____

    c. Sex on the astral planes
       is a sin. _____
       is more fulfilling than on the earth plane. _____
       does not exist. _____
       causes arguments at home. _____

    d. The following environmental conditions are important:
       Temperature _____
       Security _____
       Level of light _____
       Level of noise _____

2. Detail your first twilight-zone astral travel.

   _____

   _____

   _____

   _____

3. Describe the aka thread or cord connection to your astral body.

   _____

   _____

4. Describe your projection key signal.

_____

_____

For statistical reasons, please keep your answers informative and concise, and within the lines and format given on this page. If you need more space, of course use another sheet. Your answers are being compared to the work of other subjects. Please note that all answers are kept strictly confidential.

Appendix A
QUESTIONNAIRE

AFTER YOUR FIRST SUCCESSFUL ASTRAL PROJECTIONS

A. Give two ways in which you know you were projecting.

   1. _____

      _____

   2. _____

      _____

B. Describe the Defined Urgent Necessity you used to get out.

C. Fill in the following facts:

     Time _____   Date _____

     Moon Phase Between new and full ☐   Close to full ☐
                   Between full and new ☐   Close to new ☐
     Tick one of the above moon-phase boxes.

     Were you hungry ☐ sexually dissatisfied ☐ ?
     Tick one of the above non-homeostatic conditions.

D. Give any information you can on other variables that may have contributed to the success of your astral projections.

For statistical reasons, please keep your answers informative and concise, and within the lines and format given on this page. If you need more space, of course use another sheet. Your answers are being compared to the work of other subjects. Please note that all answers are kept strictly confidential.

QUESTIONNAIRE

AFTER YOUR FIRST ASTRAL TRIP IN TIME

A. Project to the site of the Apollo 13 moon landing. Is the American flag still flying? Yes ☐ No ☐ Tick one.

B. Arrange with a friend to do a psychic dream experiment. Tell him you are going to send him a dream. On the arranged night, astrally project, guide his 'I' from its body, and give your friend's 'Me' the vision of a red, red rose. Have him write down what he remembers of his dreams on the night in question. Establish in your own mind whether his report means success or failure. Remember not only that you should grade it a success if he actually saw a rose, but also if he had a highly romantic-style dream or other dream involving directly related symbology.

Forward to the School your friend's description of his dream and your analysis of it.

C. Astrally project forward to about the 2300 CE[5] time period.
Tell us how the following appear to you:
Colours _____
Sounds _____
Smells _____

D. Astrally project back to about 1600 CE.
Tell us how the following appear to you:
Colours _____
Sounds _____
Smells _____

For statistical reasons, please keep your answers informative and concise, and within the lines and format given on this page. If you need more space, of course use another sheet. Your answers are being compared to the work of other subjects. Please note that all answers are kept strictly confidential.

Appendix A

QUESTIONNAIRE

AFTER YOUR FIFTH TRIP TO THE SPIRITUAL REALMS

A. To help us define your cultural matrix, please complete the following.

Ethnic heritage _____ Position in society _____

The culture you most closely identify with _____

Place of birth _____

If you changed countries, at what age? _____

B. How many realms have you actually entered? ____

C. In as few words as possible, describe your view of Gateway 4.

_____

_____

_____

D. In as few words as possible, describe your view of Gateway 5.

_____

_____

_____

E. Please describe the changes that have come into your life as a result of taking this course. (If you also wish to describe the difficulties you may have had along the path or in understanding the course, you may do so.)

_____

_____

_____

_____

_____

_____

_____

_____

_____

For statistical reasons, please keep your answers informative and concise, and within the lines and format given on this page. If you need more space, of course use another sheet. Your answers are being compared to the work of other subjects. Please note that all answers are kept strictly confidential.

APPENDIX B

STATISTICAL ANALYSIS TABLES

Statistical Analysis of Questionnaires Returned by Researchers for the Canterbury Institute and Students of the School of Wicca

Canterbury Institute

Total number of researchers enrolled in programme	1,250
Number of questionnaires analysed	1,011
Dropouts:	
a) moved, no forwarding address	27
b) died	4
c) dropped out because of marital problems	31
d) lost interest because couldn't instantly make it work	177

School of Wicca

Total number of enrolled students	317
Number of questionnaires analysed	186
Dropouts:	
a) moved, no forwarding address	3
b) dropped out because of marital problems	11
c) lost interest because couldn't instantly make it work	23
Still in progress	94

Total Questionnaires Analysed

Only complete sets of questionnaires were analysed. Those who did not complete the work, and those still in the midst of a course, were eliminated.

Total student and researcher questionnaires analysed	1,197
Female	721
Male	476

	Success Per cent	Student Numbers
Successful in astral travel to the here-now	91	1,101
Successful in astral travel to the cosmic here-now	90	1,091
Successful in astral travel in the here-now and time	77	932
Successful in all phases of astral travel	72	869

If the 'couldn't make it work' dropouts are included in the percentages, the over-all success rate drops from 72% to 63% for those who were successful in all phases of astral travel. The rate for those who learned to travel in the here-now drops from an amazing 91% to 78%.

In the success rate females at 52% fared slightly better than males at 48%. Conversely in the dropout category females dropped out more often at 65% than males at 35%.

The following tables are in percentages. The columns headed 'A' are percentages that include the dropouts. Columns headed 'S' are for all students and researchers who completed the work, even though they were not totally successful.

Religious Background

	A	S
Average Christian	61	39
Fundamental Christian	12	4
Catholic	20	14
Wiccan or Pagan	8	12
Other	1	41

Social Class (the subject's own evaluation)

	A	S
Working class	45	44
Middle class	51	52
Upper class	4	4

Educational Background

	A	S
Grade school	4	2
Some high school	15	15
High school graduate	22	22
Some college	29	30
College graduate	20	21
Advanced degree	10	10

The percentages reflect the highest level the students attained. The number of people with higher degrees who are interested in the occult was further analysed because in the general population of the two countries (England and America) the population of persons with advanced degrees in the general public is less than 1%. It was found that the high interest rate was not biased by our advertising or our method of obtaining researchers or students.

Cultural Background

	A	S
Celtic	51	69
Latin	19	11
Norse	25	25
Other	5	5

Most Successful Urgent Necessity

	S
To find or see a relative	45
To find a new companion	18
Money	23
Answer a question	11
Other	3

Projection Key Signal

	S
Throbbing between eyes	22

White light	31
Tickling in genitalia	9
Tickling in solar plexus	11
Clock stopped or slowed	16
Other	11

Aka Thread

Among those who first separated by forming an astral double.

	S
Cord attached	
a) between shoulders	37
b) to solar plexus	26
c) to heels	18
No cord sensed	19

Sexual Activity Level

Frequency of Orgasms	A	S
More than 1 per day	1	0
1 per day	10	5
1 each 2–4 days	60	80
Less than 1 per 5 days	19	15

Only 271 responses were received to this portion of the questionnaires. All age groups are included. The averaging may give a distorted statistic, because the success group tended to cyclical bursts of sexual activity wherein they maintained an average of more than one per day for a short period.

Dream Control Success Rate

	S
Saw roses	45
Romantic dream	20
Unsuccessful	35

Reports Agreeing with Descriptive Material Supplied

Realm

Here-now	90
Here-now Guidance	75
Zonal Time	80
Cosmic Here-now	92
Cultural	65
Cultural Guidance	60
Gateway 5	95

The lowering level of agreement with the material as the higher levels were approached may be due to the variability of the realms. Subjects having strong opinions from prior reading would influence the realms towards their expectation. The Institute was most pleased at the total concurrence (95%) with their description of Gateway 5.

Zonal Time came up with the most surprising statistic: that is, 14% found that in their reality construct colours grew brighter and sounds got more vibrant as they went back in time and the mistiness was experienced as they went forward in time. The immutability of time past was not changed by this reversal.

Age Profile

	A	S
16–25	20	22
26–35	26	30
36–55	31	19
56 and over	23	29

The drop off in percentages in the successful group for the 36–55 age group is assumed to be because they were more often distracted from the work.

Pattern of Dwelling Location

	A	S
Urban	31	29
Suburban	27	20
Rural	34	50
Mobile	8	1

The large mobile loss was correlated more with 'moved, no forwarding address' dropouts rather than with any lack of success on the part of the mobile population who did stay in contact.

Length of Time Interested in the Occult

	A	S
Less than 1 year	6	11
1–5 years	72	75
more than 6 years	22	14

Comments from Letters

In the case of most students and researchers a large volume of correspondence passed between the instructor and the worker. Some of the characteristics of the workers in their own words were repeated so often as to form a pattern. Under the characteristics mentioned most, we find:

a) happy childhood

b) a loner (Most of the workers had tried marriage once. Some were still happily married to their first spouse, but most preferred a spouse who did not crowd them so they could stay loners.)

c) withdrawn, bookish, slightly introverted were common adjectives that the workers used in describing themselves.

Every student and researcher, even those who dropped out early in the course work, reported that they gained immeasurable serenity from participating. Many had had prior astral or *déjà vu* experiences, and the course reassured them that they were not peculiar.

When asked why they took the course, many responded that it was to gain knowledge, but an equally large group responded that they hoped that it would bring their lives into control. This may be a sign of the times and only longer term research will reveal whether this is true.

Summary

In general both the Institute and the School were most encouraged by the high percentages of successful astral travel, especially because these percentages did not seem to be dependent on cultural background or educational attainments. The course material was written in a somewhat scholarly manner, and this fact may have discouraged those with less developed language skills. The change of religious affiliation from the more formal religions to loosely structured groups seems mainly due to the lack of knowledge of the occult on the part of priests and ministers of traditional churches. In some cases the Institute's instructors simply gave up when faced with exhortations that they be 'saved' before attempting to teach this subject matter.

The shift from urban to rural in the success group surprised the Institute; however, in second-guessing this result it should have been obvious that there are far less distractions, both on the mundane and on the psychic level, in the country.

Bibliography

The following titles are typical of the many books used as reference material for parts of the text. The reader realizes already that most of the material came from the Canterbury Institute's research studies. These books are therefore supplied as optional reading so that the dedicated researcher can see that each contains a hint of the truth. The Canterbury Institute in no way claims that it has the full and ultimate truth, but the researchers do sincerely feel that they are closer than any single author has ever been.

Allegro, J., *Sacred Mushroom and the Cross*, Bantam.

Bestic, A., *Praise the Lord and Pass the Contribution*, Taplinger.

Carrington, H., *Your Psychic Powers*, Samuel Weiser.

Cerminara, G., *Many Mansions*, Signet.

Crookall, Robert, *Techniques of Astral Projection*, Aquarian.

Fodor, N., *The Haunted Mind*, Tandem.

Fox, O., *Astral Projection*, University Books.

Grant, J. & Kelsey, D., *Many Lifetimes*.

Gray, Eden, *The Tarot Revealed*, Bell Publishing Company.

Hill, N., *Think and Grow Rich*, Crest.

Howe, E.G., *Mind of the Druid*, Samuel Weiser.

MacNitt, R.D., *How to Use Astral Power*, Parker Publishing Company.

Monroe, Robert, *Journeys Out of the Body*, Anchor Press.

Montgomery, R., *A World Beyond*, Coward McCann and Geohegan.

Moser, Robert, *Mental and Astral Projection*, Esoteric Publications.

Parkinson, C., *Parkinson's Law*, John Murray.

Peter, L. & Hull, R., *The Peter Principle*, Souvenir Press.

Petersen, M., *Which Church Is Right?*, Deseret News Press.

Ponce, Charles, *Kabbalah (Sephiroth)*, Garnstone Press.

Puharich, A., *Sacred Mushroom, Key to Eternity*, Doubleday.

Roberts, Jane, *The Seth Material*, Prentice Hall.

Roberts, Jane, *Seth Speaks*, Prentice Hall.

Stearn, J., *Yoga, Youth, and Reincarnation*, Doubleday.

Steiger, Brad, *Other Lives*, Hawthorn.

Stevenson, I., *Twenty Cases Suggestive of Reincarnation*, Bantam.

Townsend, R., *Up the Organization*, Fawcett Crest.